Contents

Notes on the Authors

David Pearce is Professor of Economics at University College London; Associate Director of the London Environmental Economics Centre; and Director-Designate of the Centre for Social and Economic Research on the Global Environment.

Edward Barbier is Director of the London Environmental Economics Centre, and Senior Researcher at the International Institute for Environment and Development.

Anil Markandya is Reader in Economics at University College London, and Associate Director of the London Environmental Economics Centre.

Scott Barrett is Assistant Professor of Economics at the London Business School, and an Associate Fellow of the London Environmental Economics Centre.

R. Kerry Turner is Senior Lecturer in Environmental Economics, University of East Anglia; Executive Director-Designate of the Centre for Social and Economic Research on the Global Environment; Director of the Environmental Appraisal Group; and Associate Fellow of the London Environmental Economics Centre.

Timothy Swanson is Lecturer in Economics and Law at University College London, and Associate Fellow of the London Environmental Economics Centre.

The main author responsibility for the chapters in *Blueprint 2* is as follows: Chapters 1, 2 and general editor – David Pearce; Chapter 3 – Scott Barrett; Chapters 4 and 5 – Anil Markandya; Chapter 6 – Ed Barbier; Chapter 7 – David Pearce; Chapter 8 – Ed Barbier; Chapter 9 – R. Kerry Turner; Chapter 10 – Tim Swanson; Chapter 11 – R. Kerry Turner.

Preface

"Son of Blueprint", "Blueprint 2", or plain "Blue 2", as it is affectionately known, is a sequel to *Blueprint for a Green Economy* (Earthscan, London) which was published in September 1989. *Blueprint for a Green Economy*'s theme was that economics can and should come to the aid of environmental policy. Properly interpreted, economics provides a potentially powerful defence of conservation and a novel array of weapons for correcting environmental degradation. Moreover, it offers the prospect of doing it all rather more efficiently than traditional approaches based on "command and control". *Blueprint 2* extends this message to the problems of the global economy – climate change, ozone "holes", tropical deforestation, and resource loss in the developing world.

The original *Blueprint* team (Pearce, Markandya, Barbier) has been joined by three more – Scott Barrett, Tim Swanson and R. Kerry Turner. We are grateful for their assistance. The message is similar to that of *Blueprint for a Green Economy* but not, we hope, monotonous. *Blueprint for a Green Economy* was originally prepared as a report for the UK Department of the Environment. Its remit was to dwell on the meaning of the term "sustainable development", which had been advanced, though not introduced, by the Brundtland Commission's *Our Common Future* in 1987.[1] Some media mythology grew up round the circumstances of *Blueprint for a Green Economy*'s publication. It was supposed to have been rejected by one Secretary of State and rescued from oblivion by another; loved by some and suppressed by others in Whitehall.

Whatever reporters' imaginations, the reality was:

(a) *Blueprint for a Green Economy* was commissioned in December 1988 by the Department of the Environment and was designed to advise government if there was a consensus meaning to the term "sustainable development". The rest of the terms of reference related to the implications of sustainable development for the measurement of economic progress and the appraisal of projects and policies;

(b) the chapters in *Blueprint for a Green Economy* on "valuing the environment" and "market-based incentives" (green taxes, etc.) were *not* commissioned by anyone. Along with the chapter on "discounting the future", they were added because one of us (DWP) thought the report told an incomplete story. Ironically, the valuation and incentives chapters caused most of the fuss;

(c) although we knew there was provision for possible publication, it was not our original intention to publish the report. The publicity attached to a small press conference in August 1989 came as a complete surprise;

(d) the rumours of suppression and resurrection were always exactly that – rumours. We never found any evidence to support them. But if they added to the sales, we are pleased for the publishers!

"Blue 2" continues the story. There is still a lot more to say.

DWP, AM, EB

Notes

1. World Commission on Environment and Development, *Our Common Future*, Oxford University Press, Oxford, 1987.

Acknowledgements

Blueprint for a Green Economy was a fairly lonesome affair. Not so "Blue 2". The London Environmental Economics Centre (LEEC) has acted as a focus for extensive discussion on local, national, international and global environmental issues. We are deeply indebted to the governments of Sweden, Norway and the Netherlands, who have shown consistent faith in LEEC by providing its core funding. To our friends and sponsors – the Swedish International Development Authority (SIDA), the Norwegian Ministry of Foreign Affairs, and the Dutch Ministry of Housing, Planning and Environment – we express heartfelt thanks.

Neil Middleton, Kate Griffin and Jonathan Sinclair-Wilson of Earthscan have been unstintingly supportive, and neither "Blue 1" nor "Blue 2" would have made it without them – least of all "Blue 1", which was actually published in twenty-one days. Jo Burgess was an integral part of "Blue 1" and we are delighted to acknowledge her contribution fully in "Blue 2". Richard Sandbrook presides over the International Institute for Environment and Development (IIED), of which LEEC is a part. He has never wavered in his support of LEEC, or in his belief in the role of environmental economics in the development debate. To him we are especially grateful.

In between repeated "fixes" of Botswana and Zimbabwe, Sue Pearce has read the manuscript, scorned our grammatical skills and generally improved things all round. Many, many others have exerted a strong influence on our work. We thank them all and hope we have not misinterpreted them.

DWP, AM, EB

1

Introduction

David Pearce

Blueprint for a Green Economy

The central messages of *Blueprint 1* were:

(a) sustainable development is readily interpretable as non-declining human welfare over time – that is, a development path that makes people better off today but makes people tomorrow have a lower "standard of living" is not "sustainable". This is consistent with the Brundtland definition that sustainable development means making sure that development "meets the needs of the present without compromising the ability of future generations to meet their own needs";[1]

(b) the *conditions* for achieving sustainable development include the requirement that future generations should be compensated for damage done by current generations – e.g. through global warming;

(c) compensation is best secured by leaving the next generation a stock of capital assets no less than the stock we have now (the "constant capital" requirement). This enables the next generation to achieve the same level of human welfare (at least) as the current generation. If they fail to do this, the responsibility is theirs, since they have inherited the same "productive potential" as was available to the previous generation;

(d) the capital in question is both "man-made" (Km) and "natural" (Kn). Natural capital refers to environmental assets;

(e) the requirement to keep the *total* of capital (Km + Kn) constant is consistent with "running down" natural capital –

i.e. with environmental degradation – so long as Km and Kn are readily substitutable for each other. Thus, the "constant capital" rule is consistent with removing the Amazon forest so long as the proceeds from this activity are reinvested to build up some other form of capital;

(f) the constant capital rule requires that environmental assets be *valued* in the same way as man-made assets, otherwise we cannot know if we are on a "sustainable development path". We cannot know if overall capital is constant in the Amazon deforestation case unless we know the value of the services and functions that we surrender when it is lost. To put it another way: valuation is essential if we are to "trade off" forms of capital. This is the relevance of valuation; nor is there any escape from it. We "trade off" either explicitly, as *Blueprint 1* argued, or implicitly, since all decisions imply valuations;[2]

(g) but careful inspection of the values of natural capital (i.e. looking at what environmental assets do for us) will show that the trade-off has been biased in favour of eliminating or degrading those assets in favour of either "consuming" the proceeds (i.e. not reinvesting at all) or investing too readily in man-made assets. Very simply, if the "true" value of the environment were known, we would not degrade it as much;

(h) for some environmental assets, which we termed "critical capital", there is no question of an acceptable trade-off. Once allowance is made for the high *values* of natural capital, for the *uncertainty* surrounding the functions and benefits of natural capital, and for the fact that, once eliminated, the effects are *irreversible*, then there is a strong case for a precautionary approach in which the bias is towards conserving *natural capital*. It is in this sense that environmental economics offers a rationale for even greater protection of the environment than is conventionally thought;

(i) the *instruments* for securing sustainable development include the traditional "standard-setting" regulatory approach (which we called "command and control" – cac) *and* a panoply of measures which make use of the marketplace. These "market-based instruments" (MBIS) include taxes on emissions and discharges, deposit-refund systems and tradeable emission and resource-use permits. MBIS are more powerful than CAC because (i) they keep down the costs of complying with regulations; (ii) they act as a continuous "irritant" to the polluter, who therefore has a repeated incentive to avoid the MBI by introducing cleaner and cleaner technology; (iii) the consumer has a clear incentive to avoid polluting products because their prices will be higher than clean products (other things being equal); (iv) environmental taxes can be used in a "fiscally neutral" way to reduce other distorting taxes in the economy;

(j) the measures of economic progress based on "GNP" (Gross National Product) need to be changed because GNP fails to measure the true "standard of living". It largely ignores environmental assets and treats them as if they have a zero or near-zero price. (And if something is underpriced, too much of it will be consumed.) But the first priority is to construct environmental and economic indicators that show the links between economy and environment. Adjusting the national accounts (which compute the GNP) is expensive and not as high a priority as constructing "environment-economy indicators";

(k) "cost-benefit thinking" would greatly enhance the chances of conservation competing with "development" on equal terms and, indeed, would generally improve the quality of decision-making.

Critiques of Blueprint

Few critiques of *Blueprint* were published. The criticisms that were either printed or appeared several times are dealt with below. Some potentially sensible critiques were marred by false assumptions about the political bias of *Blueprint* – mainly, it seemed, because advocacy of market-based environmental policy was taken to mean advocacy of free markets. This is an inexcusable interpretation. Other critiques were remarkable for the inverse relationship between the vehemence of the criticism and the familiarity of the critic with what is now an enormous literature in environmental economics. This was nowhere more evident than in the objections to "valuing the environment" One journal published a breathtaking demonstration of the inverse rule, requested a reply from us and then refused to publish the reply![3]

A few of the more general criticisms were:

(a) *The ideas in Blueprint 1 were not new.* We never said they were, although some of the sections on sustainability and the way in which one might modify cost-benefit appraisal were in fact worked out by us.[4] What we tried to do was to draw together the various strands of environmental economics – a subject with a history of rapid development over the last twenty-five years – and apply them to the environmental problems of modern economies. One politician summed it up by saying that we had "told a coherent story in a language non-economists could understand". A few economists seemed surprised that it was necessary to convey well-established doctrine in this way, a reflection more on their political naiveté than anything else. Some critics also seemed to think we had only just discovered environmental economics – two of the original authors were writing in the field of environmental economics in the early 1970s.

(b) *It isn't possible to "value" the environment.* The idea of trying to put a monetary value on the services generated by environmental assets offended a number of people. "Monetization" does indeed raise many interesting problems, but many of them would be avoided if a more careful look was taken at what economists are actually doing when they attach money values. They are not "valuing the environment" in itself. They are valuing individual human preferences *for* (or against) the flow of services from the environment. It is perfectly possible to argue that there are "other" values, perhaps "value in things" rather than "value of things". As yet, no operational rules for decision-makers seem to have emerged from the "value in things" literature. If everything has a right to being, then the problem of "trading off" rights is unavoidable – something philosophers pointed out long ago. If some rights are more important than others (which raises the issue of how we decide that), then there are similarities perhaps with our concept of "critical natural capital".

Some critics suggested that the environment is "beyond price". If this means that individuals have no preferences for or against environmental services, it is patently false. If it means that we cannot *measure* those preferences, that is a moot point, but we do of course measure other preferences in money terms every second of the day. That is what share prices or supermarket prices are. Why is the environment different? The absence of markets in environmental services creates a *practical* problem of measurement – i.e. one of finding out what people preferences actually are in a context where there are no apparent markets – but it does not generate a *conceptual* problem of measurement.

Perhaps "beyond price" means that the environment is *infinitely* valued. Some functions of critical natural capital may indeed have very high values, since they support life itself and are not substitutable.[5] But if environmental assets were of infinite value we would never allow any form of environmental degradation, yet no society devotes all of its GNP to environmental protection. OECD countries typically spend 1–2 per cent of their GNP on it. We would agree that they should spend more, and that what they spend should be spent efficiently, but that conclusion reflects a belief about the economic value of the environment (where "economic" here means the role of the environment in satisfying human preferences – it does *not* mean "commercial"). When people say the environment has "infinite" value, we suspect they mean either that *their* values are very high, or that environmental assets somehow lie outside the realm of money values. We do not dispute the former interpretation which, of course, would show up in the valuation procedures we recommended. The second poses as many problems as it is supposed to solve since, quite clearly, people do have preferences for environmental services and do express them in money terms – otherwise it would be difficult to explain much of the behaviour towards the environment. Chapter 11 addresses this issue in more detail.

(c) *Environmental taxes will hurt the poor*. A common objection to environmental taxes is that they are held to be "regressive" – i.e. the tax imposes a larger proportionate burden on low-income groups than it does on higher-income groups. This is especially true of taxes on energy, and thus of "carbon" taxes. Box 1.1 illustrates the distributional incidence of a hypothetical introduction of 15 per cent value added tax (VAT) on domestic fuel. The effects of the tax are simulated

---

Box 1.1 **The Regressive Incidence of a Tax on Energy Consumption**

Change in fuel consumption, by decile of gross income

Decile of gross income	Change in fuel consump- tion fuel (%)	Change in tax pre-response (£ per week)	Change in tax paid (£ per week)	Change in tax paid (as % of spending)
Lowest	−9.61	1.19	1.08	1.80
2	−9.50	1.51	1.36	1.54
3	−8.26	1.56	1.41	1.16
4	−6.83	1.68	1.49	0.93
5	−4.84	1.72	1.49	0.74
6	−4.11	1.68	1.44	0.67
7	−3.43	1.85	1.57	0.62
8	−1.97	1.90	1.59	0.55
9	−0.06	2.06	1.69	0.48
Highest	+1.09	2.53	2.05	0.42
Average	−4.12	1.77	1.52	0.68

The tax assumed is a 15% VAT on domestic fuel. The effects on income groups ranging from the lowest 10% to the highest 10% is shown.

Source: P. Johnson, S. Mckay and S. Smith, *The Distributional Consequences of Environmental Taxes*, Institute for Fiscal Studies, London, July 1990.

with a Simulation Program for Indirect Taxation (SPIT) developed by the Institute for Fiscal Studies in London. The main results are:

(i) that the tax would raise revenues of around £1.7 billion for government;

(ii) that fuel consumption would fall by only 4 per cent owing to the "inelasticity" of demand for fuel in the household sector;

(iii) that the poorest household would pay around £1 per week extra in tax and the richest around £2 per week. As a proportion of household spending, these extra taxes amount to 1.8 per cent of the spending of the lowest-income household, and 0.4 per cent of the highest-income household's spending. That is, the proportionate burden is high for low-income groups.

It appears to be true, then, that environmental taxes, especially taxes on energy, will tend to have a regressive incidence. But is this the whole story?

There are two problems with the analysis so far. First, it makes no reference to the context of the tax. If the aim is to achieve, say, a carbon dioxide emission target, then the alternative to the tax would be *some other measure*. It is not a case of choosing between the tax and doing nothing. Therefore, before we can say anything conclusive about the incidence of the tax, we need to know what the incidence of the price impacts of any other measure would be. Any regulation imposes costs on producers, and some of these costs are passed on to the consumer. What we need to know is the *differential* impact of a CAC-type regulation and the tax. That information is not conveyed in Box 1.1.

The second problem is that the analysis assumes that revenues are kept by the government, but that need not be the case. Indeed, one of the attractions of environmental taxes is that they can be treated in a "fiscally neutral" way. This means that the revenue raised can be returned to the economy in some other way. The justification for this is twofold: first, the tax is an *incentive* tax. It is designed to alter behaviour, in this case the behaviour of consumers of fuel; it is not concerned with raising revenues for government. Second, revenues could be returned by cutting other taxes that have a distortionary effect on effort or enterprise – e.g. income tax or corporation tax. The environmental tax thus achieves two objectives: reducing pollution and improving the efficiency of the economy. In the current context, of course, the revenues could be returned in the form of compensation to low-income households. When this is done we need to determine what offsetting expenditures these low-income groups would make on energy. That is, the initial tax reduces their consumption, but raising their incomes to compensate them will mean that they will increase their energy consumption compared to the after-tax situation. The study from which Box 1.1 is taken shows how various policies for compensation could be devised. Several studies show that significant taxes on the carbon content of fuels would (a) raise very large revenues for government; (b) have initially dramatic regressive impacts, but (c) the regressive impacts can be offset with redistributive measures; and (d) the level of CO_2 emissions can be reduced substantially.[6]

(d) *"The polluter pays" means "the consumer pays"*. Since pollution taxes raise the costs of the polluter, some of these increased costs are passed on to consumers. Some critics seemed to think that this was a criticism of the polluter pays principle, but in fact it is exactly what should happen. The pollution tax signals to the polluter that he or she should change to a cleaner technology. If this change is made, the polluter will, of course, avoid the pollution tax, but bear the costs of the cleaner technology. If he or she chooses to pay the tax, then some of the tax burden is passed on to consumers. Note that *all* the tax cannot be passed on, as some people seem to think, because that would imply that consumers are totally insensitive to price. Typically, demand varies with price, so some of the tax burden must be borne by the polluter. The consumer faces higher prices as a result of the tax – though the extent of these higher prices depends on what is done with the tax revenues (see above). The consumer thus gets a signal that polluting products are dearer than less polluting ones. This gives the added incentive to the polluter to change technology and keep prices down in the marketplace, otherwise he or she loses customers. Consumer prices are *meant* to rise under the polluter pays principle. Indeed, it is odd to think of the polluter as being the industrialist only. We are all polluters. We the consumers send signals to industry as to what it is we want to buy. Our demands therefore contribute to the "pollution profile" of the economy.

(e) *Pollution taxes impair competitiveness*. Industry is rightly concerned that there should be a "level playing field" with respect to environmental regulation. If industry A bears the cost of a regulation but B does not, then B will gain a competitive edge over A. However, while this criticism is understandable, it overexaggerates the problems with environmental taxes. First, it assumes that the alternative to the tax is doing nothing, which is not the case. Some other form of regulation will occur and that will also raise costs, as previously discussed. Second, tax revenues can, as we have seen, be used to offset other distortionary taxes such as corporation tax. An environmental tax combined with a reduced corporation tax could be attractive to industry. (Note that with the alternative regulation based on CAC, this option is not open.) Third, the context of a number of environmental taxes will be an international one. A carbon tax, for example, is likely to be introduced on a significant scale only if it is introduced by a number of countries acting together, or in a context where those countries all agree they will do *something* about CO_2 emissions.

Blueprint 2

Any environmental policy faces formidable practical problems of implementation. The argument in *Blueprint 1* was that the use of MBIS in a "mixed" system of MBIS and CAC (we never argued for MBIS alone, contrary to what some critics thought) is more efficient than a system based on CAC alone. This is especially important at a time when environmental regulation is likely to become stricter, not laxer. The theme of *Blueprint 2* is that this conclusion holds not just for domestic environmental policy, *but for global environmental policy as well*. The rest of the book is devoted to this theme.

Notes

1. World Commission on Environment and Development, *Our Common Future*, Oxford University Press, Oxford, 1987, p. 8.
2. This elementary point appears to have escaped most of the critics of valuation.
3. The journal in question is called *International Environmental Affairs*. Our reply to the review is available on request.
4. These have since be extended more formally. See D. W. Pearce, A. Markandya and E. Barbier, "Environmental Sustainability and Cost-Benefit Analysis", *Environment and Planning* Series A, vol. 22, 1990, pp. 1259–66.
5. This might be an economic interpretation of the "Gaia hypothesis", for example. See J. Lovelock, *Gaia: A New Look at Life on Earth*, Oxford University Press, Oxford, 1979.
6. See, for example, E. Symons, J. Proops and P. Gay, "Carbon Taxes, Consumer Demand and Carbon Dioxide Emission: A Simulation Analysis for the UK", Department of Economics and Management Science, University of Keele, Keele, November 1990.

2

The Global Commons

David Pearce

"Blueprint" and the World Economy

Blueprint for a Green Economy did discuss some global issues such as climatic change and the role that a carbon tax might play in controlling global warming, but by and large it was concerned with the problem of a single economy. *Blueprint 2* quite explicitly looks at international and global environmental problems. Our argument is that "green economics" has as large a role to play in containing these formidable issues as it has in dealing with nationally confined environmental damage. Indeed, it is all the more important to make use of the economic approach because of the very large costs that may eventually be involved in managing the "global commons" such as the atmosphere and the oceans. Two types of cost are likely to be involved. First, the rich nations of the world will need to "put their own house in order" in respect of pollution and excessive resource use. Second, in order to persuade the developing world to join forces to combat major problems such as tropical deforestation and global warming, it will be necessary to transfer resources from rich to poor countries. In this sense, the rich countries of the world must pay twice: once to "clean up" the environmental degradation they have created through environmentally insensitive growth, and twice to *prevent* the developing world engaging in yet further environmental destruction. Additionally, existing degradation in the developing world has to be addressed.

Here, then, is one argument why the process of tackling environmental degradation cannot be resolved by "no growth" policies in the rich world. No growth combined with the resource transfers that will have to take place means a marked diminution in the material standard of living for the average person in the developed world. Some environmentalists argue in favour of this very effect and, of course, tend also to believe that this decline in material standards will be accompanied by an increase in "non-material" welfare. That may prove to be true, but the view of what we call green economics is that this process is neither necessary nor desirable. While we wait for the world to become "spiritually green", much more of it will be lost and degraded. We can act before then by driving a "wedge" between economic growth and the environment, a wedge that uncouples the economic growth process's impact on the environment. To put it another way: if we can alter the *ratio* of growth to environmental impact, we can afford to grow and generate the resources that are needed to alter the growth process in the developing world so that the same environmental mistakes are not made. The wedge can be regulation of the CAC type but, for the reasons we advanced in *Blueprint 1*, we believe the use of a market-based approach is far more efficient.

What are the global threats? By now most people are familiar with them. They include the depletion of the ozone layer through excessive use of chlorofluorocarbons (CFCs), the possibility of global warming through the excess emission of "greenhouse gases", loss of the world's biological diversity and the loss of uniquely wonderful environmental assets such as tropical forests. Why do these things matter? This may seem an odd question to ask. To many people it is simply *wrong* to eliminate species, burn forests, degrade rangelands and heat up the world. Probably most of the authors of this volume would agree. But it is also wrong to deprive people of their livelihoods, and simply "banning" certain economic activity, forbidding use of some natural resources, or "mothballing" what is to be conserved create as many problems as they resolve.[1] Instead, what is required is the design of an *incentive system* which both conserves the resource and yet removes or modifies the underlying factors giving rise to environmental loss. In other words, designing policies without looking at the *causes* of environmental degradation is a high-risk and probably self-defeating approach.

The rest of this chapter introduces some of the issues involved in an economic analysis of global problems.

Global Warming

There is extensive *scientific* uncertainty about the nature of global warming. There is also *economic* uncertainty, because we cannot be sure what the *impacts* will be, nor even how humans will respond. If it is all so uncertain, why bother to do anything? In *Blueprint 1* we drew attention to several features of the global warming problem. First, the *scale* of the problem could be very large, perhaps of an order that would merit terms like "catastrophe". Second, if induced warming occurs it will be *irreversible*. If future generations do not like a warmed-up world, there is little they can do about it. Third, as we have noted, the consequences are *uncertain*. It is this *combination* of features that justifies precautionary action now rather than later. If global warming turns out to be "true", then a failure to take action now will mean bigger sacrifices for the next generation. That, it will be recalled, is inconsistent with the requirements of sustainable development – namely, that the current generation should not prosper at the expense of the next generation, and so on. If global warming turns out to be false, the current generation will have sacrificed some benefit. If, of course, that sacrifice is large, then it is wholly legitimate to look at the "trade-off" between present and future and decide on the best evidence available. If the current generation stands to sacrifice comparatively little, then the bias towards a precautionary approach (because of uncertainty, irreversibility and "scale") is further strengthened.

The United Nations Intergovernmental Panel on Climate Change (IPCC) suggests [Box 2.1] that global mean temperatures may rise, from now on, at somewhere between 0.2°C and 0.5°C per decade if we do nothing – i.e. "business as usual". The best estimate is 0.3°C per decade. Under alternative scenarios in which there are controls on greenhouse gas emissions, the temperature increases are less – at 0.2°C per decade for scenario B, in which natural gas is substituted for higher carbon fuels, deforestation is halted, and substantial energy-efficiency measures

Box 2.1   **Global Warming Scenarios According to IPCC**

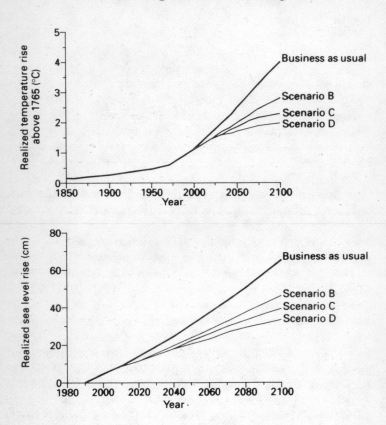

are introduced; and at 0.1°C or just above it for scenarios D and C respectively, in which controls are even more stringent and renewable energy, including nuclear power, takes substantial shares of the energy market by the middle of the next century. There are, of course, corresponding sea level rises for these scenarios, as Box 2.1 shows.

The greenhouse gases giving rise to global warming are

Box 2.2 **The Greenhouse Gases**

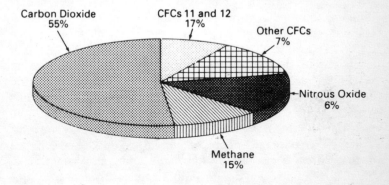

CO$_2$, CFCs, methane, nitrous oxide, and ozone [Box 2.2]. The contribution made by ozone is not very clear at the moment.

The IPCC scenarios do not, in themselves, tell us anything about the need for policy. For all we know, these temperature and sea level rises are associated with levels of damage that we can accommodate. Moreover, the likely damages need to be compared to the costs of taking action. The only studies we have to date which compare costs and benefits do not suggest any need for dramatic concern. For example, Professor Nordhaus of Yale University suggests that a comparison of costs and benefits suggests an "optimal" cutback of some 17 per cent off the combined total of greenhouse gas emissions.[2] But because it is more cost-effective to cut back on chlorofluorocarbons (CFCs), which have a much higher global warming impact per unit of emission than CO$_2$, much of this suggested reduction comes from reducing CFCs. It is necessary on this analysis to reduce CO$_2$ by only 6 per cent. But this is 6 per cent off a baseline trend – that is, we can allow CO$_2$ to rise so long as we keep it to 6 per cent below the rise that would have occurred without any controls. This is in fact an extremely modest level of CO$_2$ control.

If either the damage done by global warming is greater than Nordhaus suggests, or if the costs of cutting back on emissions are lower than he suggests, we would have a rationale for some stronger global warming medicine. There are some reasons for thinking that the cost-benefit approach might dictate stricter controls. Some insight into this is obtained by looking at a different approach. The alternative to the cost-benefit approach is to try to detect a zone of unknown risk and then to set global warming targets which avoid that zone on the grounds that the unknown includes potentially catastrophic impacts. The "unknowability" of the risks arises from the fact that if global warming is allowed to go very far, we will pass beyond the sphere of human experience and hence beyond what is reasonably knowable about ecosystem reaction. Put simply, anything could happen if we exceed this threshold.

What might this threshold be? It has been widely suggested that we should not allow *absolute* global temperatures to rise beyond 2.5°C above "pre-industrial" levels by 2030.[3] The rationale for this is that it would contain temperature increases to below the *maximum* temperature experienced during the last several million years *in which human beings have been on the earth*.[4] To allow temperatures to rise above this level would therefore be to enter into a "zone of ignorance" which lies outside human history. Temperatures have risen around 0.5°C since 1850, so the 2.5°C maximum target is about 2°C above current temperatures. Some recent reports suggest that the absolute limit to warming should be only 1°C.[5] There also appears to be agreement that a risk-minimization policy would limit the *rate of warming* to below 0.1°C per decade. This "allowable rate of warming" is determined by the rate at which forests and other ecosystems are estimated to adapt to temperature change without severe dislocation.

The 0.1°C rate of warming limit may be compared to IPCC's best estimate that we are adding to warming at the rate of 0.3°C per decade. How the 0.1°C rate of warming target translates into allowable *emissions* depends on climate sensitivity – i.e. the rate at which warming will occur in response to increases in greenhouse gases. The IPCC suggests that the range of climate sensitivity is 1.5 to 4.5°C for a doubling of CO_2. Their best estimate of sensitivity is 2.5°C. If climate sensitivity is higher than IPCC's 2.5°C/2 × CO_2 at, say, 3.6°C, then one model suggests that CO_2 concentrations must be no higher than 400 parts per million (ppm) and the allowable cumulative emission budget no more than 200 billion tonnes from now to the year at which concentrations of CO_2 are stabilized.[6] The "carbon budget" increases to 340 billion tonnes if climate sensitivity is 3.0°C per doubling of CO_2, so we might expect over 400 billion tonnes "allowable burn" for IPCC's best estimate of 2.5°C sensitivity. Another model, with a similar concentration target of 380–400 ppm for CO_2 alone, suggests a 300-billion-tonne "budget" until the year 2100, but assumes a high climate sensitivity of 4–5.5°C.[7]

Box 2.3 offers one view of the risk-minimization argument. A hypothetical target of 0.1°C maximum warming per decade is assumed, along with a 2.5°C absolute target above pre-industrial levels. Beyond this we are into a zone of ignorance. The "damage function" may therefore take on any shape after the 0.1°C threshold is passed. Nordhaus's cost-benefit approach tends to assume that it is a function something like line A, but if the scientists are right, there could be catastrophic damage and the appropriate function may be something like line B.

To keep within the 0.1°C rate of warming we require that CO_2 concentrations never exceed a certain level. One model suggests that this is 400–500 ppm – i.e. concentrations are stabilized at this level at some future year, say 2030.[8] To achieve this, the maximum allowable cumulative emissions have to be 200–400 billion tonnes between now and the year of concentration stabilization. If this is 2030, we are therefore saying that allowable emissions should be 5–11 billion tonnes per annum compared to 6.4 to 8.3 billion tonnes now, from all sources, *and* the emission rate would have to be falling before 2030 for concentrations to be stabilized in that year.

Box 2.3   **Climate Change and the "Zone of Uncertainty"**

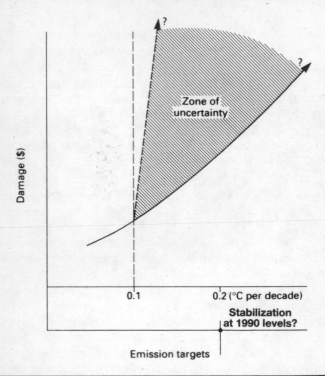

Fairly clearly, then, stabilization at *current* levels of emission would need to be introduced *immediately* if we are to avoid the zone of ignorance.

  The world's negotiators are not generally talking about immediate stabilization, although the widely mooted "Toronto target" aims for a 20 per cent reduction of CO_2 on 1988 levels by 2005, which is probably broadly equivalent. The discussion is centring on one of two targets: stabilizing CO_2 emissions at 1990 levels by 2000 or by 2005, with further reductions thereafter. Box 2.4 shows the positions of different countries in this respect as at the end of 1990. The

Box 2.4 Country Targets for Carbon Dioxide Control

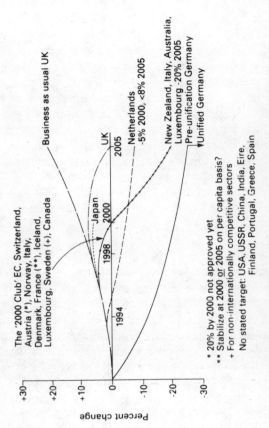

The '2000 Club' EC, Switzerland, Austria (*), Norway, Italy, Denmark, France (**), Iceland, Luxembourg, Sweden (+), Canada

Business as usual UK

Japan

UK
2005

Netherlands
-5% 2000, <8% 2005

New Zealand, Italy, Australia, Luxembourg -20% 2005
Pre-unification Germany
Unified Germany

Percent change

* 20% by 2000 not approved yet
** Stabilize at 2000 or 2005 on per capita basis?
+ For non-internationally competitive sectors
No stated target: USA, USSR, China, India, Eire, Finland, Portugal, Greece, Spain

The diagram shows different targets for different countries as at end 1990. No significance should be attached to the shapes of the curves.

USA, USSR, India and China, which between them account for 40 per cent of net CO_2 emissions, have no stated targets.[9]

Broadly speaking, the "1990 by 2000/2005" targets appear to be consistent with a warming rate of 0.2°C per decade, which puts the world substantially into the zone of ignorance. Moreover, it assumes that other countries – and especially the major polluters – will sign up to this target, or something similar. The cost-benefit approach discussed previously says little about how to behave in the zone of ignorance. It also tends to assume that the costs of abating CO_2 are not very low for the first tranche of controls. Finally, it says nothing about the benefits we can enjoy if we control CO_2 and other gases, which are quite incidental to any reduced damage from global warming. The combination of these factors suggests that the Nordhaus prescription for very limited controls on CO_2 perhaps overstates the costs of achieving CO_2 reductions, omits significant incidental benefits from CO_2 control, and perhaps underplays the extent to which risk aversion should guide policy.

Box 2.5 shows the results of one analysis of CO_2 control policy in a single country, Norway. The hypothetical mechanism used to secure the freezing of CO_2 emissions in the year 2000 is a tax on carbon fuels – i.e. a "carbon tax", in this case mainly on oil. Clearly, if Norway were to act unilaterally in reducing CO_2 emissions, and no one else followed, then no discernible gain in terms of global warming would accrue to anyone. This is because Norway accounts for only 0.2 per cent of the world's emissions of CO_2 – it cannot independently affect the world's climate. There are two forms of benefit that Norway would secure if it did decide to act alone. First, it would have made a contribution to climate control by playing its part in a global convention. Second, the act of controlling CO_2 emissions gives rise to *other* benefits for example reduced congestion, accidents, air pollution etc. – as Box 2.5 shows. In this particular case, we see that some two-thirds of the costs of control are recovered in the form of benefits unrelated to global warming.

Box 2.5   **The Costs and Benefits of Controlling Carbon Dioxide in Norway**

Scenario: Norway "freezes" CO_2 emissions at the level reached in 2000. A rising fuel tax is used to achieve the freeze. As an illustration, the price of fuel oil would be raised by 50% in 2005 and 100% in 2010.

Costs	Bn N. Krone (1986 prices) in 2010
Costs measured in terms of forgone GNP	*27.0*
"Domestic" Benefits	
Reduced forest/lake damage due to acid rain	0.1
Health improvement from reduced NO_x, SO_2, CO and particulates	7.6
Reduced corrosion	0.2
Reduced traffic accidents	2.7
Reduced traffic congestion	2.9
Reduced road damage	3.6
Reduced noise	2.1
Total domestic benefits	*19.2*
Net domestic benefits	*−7.8*
Net domestic benefits as % GNP in 2010	*−0.8*

Source: S. Glomsrod *et al.*, "Stabilization of Emissions of CO_2: A Computable General Equilibrium Assessment", Central Bureau of Statistics, Oslo, April 1990.

If the incidental benefits of CO_2 control are significant, then action on CO_2 really does not carry with it any prospect of severe social costs – at least, not as far as the initial round of targets is concerned. Further targets may, it is true, impose more significant costs on society in terms of forgone economic growth. What economic impact there is can be made even smaller by ensuring that the measures adopted are the low-cost measures that are already available, most notably in the area of energy conservation. On top of that, if the carbon tax approach to climate control were adopted, such taxes could be part of a fiscally neutral package whereby government raises revenue with the carbon tax and returns that revenue back to society in the form of reduced taxes on income and effort. In that way, we could further reduce the economic burden of climate control whilst simultaneously improving the efficiency of the economy and securing pollution reductions.

The way to behave in the context of scientific and economic uncertainty about the greenhouse effect is to adopt fairly restrictive measures on the emissions of greenhouse gases. If low-cost measures with high incidental benefits are adopted, the burden of any international agreement on CO_2 can be low. If we recognize that the *means* of securing the targets should be based on changes in the price of carbon fuels through a carbon tax, then the burden could be even less. Of course there are other ways of securing a carbon target, and we should not overlook the virtues of tradeable emission permits in this context. But the carbon tax has the virtue that the proceeds can be returned to the economy without distorting the original purpose of the tax – namely, to reduce greenhouse gas emissions.

Neither the narrow cost-benefit approach discussed above nor the risk-minimization approach appears satisfactory. It is difficult to embrace a risk-minimization approach which totally ignores the costs of avoiding unknown risks. It is difficult to square the cost-benefit approach with the dire warnings of the scientists.

Conserving the World's Biological Diversity

"Biodiversity" refers to the variety of all species of plants, animals, and micro-organisms and the ecosystems and ecological processes of which they are part. Genetic diversity is the total of genetic information. Species diversity relates to the variety of living organisms on earth. Ecosystem diversity refers to the variety of habitats and ecological processes in the biosphere. The genetic information, the stock and variety of species, and the stock and variety of ecosystems and their functions are all "natural capital". Economists are used to analysing economic processes that include man-made capital – machines, roads, buildings – and human capital – the stock of knowledge and capabilities. They are also used to analysis with some forms of natural capital – stocks of energy, trees and fish. They are perhaps only now coming to terms with the need to treat natural capital as a far more embracing term, to include both biogeochemical cycles and complete ecosystems.

As with global warming, the context for decision-making is one of uncertainty. Many of the benefits of biological diversity conservation are not known, a fact that simply reflects our limited understanding of how the world's ecosystems function. Even at the species level, science has described perhaps 1.4 million species out of an unknown total of species – at least 5 million, and maybe 30 million or more.[10] We cannot know what benefits to mankind these undescribed species will bring. As with global warming, if we allow biodiversity to be further eroded, we might be in the realms of *irreversible* losses, although we should be clear that fairly substantial reductions in natural ecosystems can occur without total biodiversity being reduced significantly. This combination of uncertainty and irreversibility is enough to tell us to be cautious and to err on the side of conservation at least until we are clearer about the threats to biodiversity in general.

Of the four features of the climatic change policy issue so far discussed –

uncertainty
irreversibility
risk of high damage
low initial costs of control

– the first two also characterize the biodiversity issue. We briefly investigate the last two – the damage done by biodiversity loss and the costs of controlling that loss.

In truth, we know little about the economic losses that ensue from reductions in biodiversity, but there is one major loss that should be recognized and for which the framework for valuation exists. Very simply, people are upset by damage to ecosystems such as tropical forests, wetlands, mangrove swamps, lakes and mountains. In economics, this is what we would record as a loss of "welfare", and welfare changes in this context are simply measured by the extent to which people prefer or do not prefer one situation over another. If an individual is upset by a loss of wildlife, his or her welfare has gone down. If the experience is of pleasure, joy, happiness from experiencing wilderness, then welfare has gone up. *Measuring* the gains and losses is an issue of *valuation*, as discussed in Chapter 1. If we can secure some measure of value of people's preferences for biodiversity, then we have the beginnings of an additional argument in favour of conservation. This is a little different from asking people's opinions, or recording protests, or taking direct action. It is a matter of measuring how much economic value there is in biodiversity. It is not a substitute for other defences of natural capital, it is an additional and potentially very powerful defence when it is allied with an analysis of how to use economic approaches to the conservation of biodiversity.

Consider the case of tropical forests. We know that they have economic value as the providers of habitat and food for indigenous peoples; we know that they yield timber and many minor non-timber products such as nuts and rattan; we know that they protect adjacent ecosystems; we know that their loss causes downstream pollution; we know that they are stores of CO_2 and that we lose that store when the forest is destroyed. They are also repositories of a form of "non-use value" known as "existence value". Existence value arises because people simply want tropical forests to exist, *regardless of any use they may make of them*. The motivations for existence value need not concern us unduly.[11] Efforts to estimate existence value are based on *contingent valuation* studies, which essentially use a "willingness to pay" questionnaire approach. No study has been carried out for tropical forests, but Box 2.6 reports estimates of average annual values per person taken from contingent valuation studies for selected animal species and natural amenities. While the studies are limited in number, there is a consistency about the values. The animal values cluster in the $5–8 range, with American national symbols – the grizzly bear

Box 2.6 Some Economic Values for Environmental Assets

Non-Use Values for Unique Natural Assets

Asset:	Value per Adult ($ mid-1980s)
Animal Species	
Bald eagle	11
Emerald shiner	4
Grizzly bear	15
Bighorn sheep	7
Whooping crane	1
Blue whale	8
Bottlenose dolphin	6
California sea otter	7
Northern elephant seal	7
Natural Amenities	
Water quality (S. Platte) river basin	4
Visibility (Grand Canyon)	22

Source: K. Semples, M. Gowen and J. Dixon, "The Validity of the Contingent Valuation Method for Estimating Non-Use Components of Preservation Values for Unique Natural Resources", paper presented to the American Agricultural Economics Association, Reno, July 1986.

and the bald eagle – in the $10–15 range. The Grand Canyon similarly has a high valuation as a piece of major national heritage, compared to the value of cleaning up a river. These figures are simply what people are willing to pay to conserve these resources. Note that this is not necessarily the same thing as saying that these resources are "worth" this much. The illicit assumption of equivalence of willingness to pay with intrinsic worth is perhaps at the root of the misunderstanding over what economists actually do when they engage in valuation studies.

Could such values be "borrowed" for tropical forests? They are unique assets, but they are (generally) not in rich countries. Allowing for this "distance" between valuer and the object of value (which applies to the blue whale as well) and the substantial worldwide interest in tropical deforestation, a figure of $8 per adult per annum would seem very conservative. Allowing for valuations by just the richest nations of the world with some 400 million adults (Western Europe, North America, Australasia), the valuation would be some $3.2 billion per annum.

The opportunity cost of forest conservation is the "development" benefits forgone. As we shall see, these may not in fact be greater than the benefits of sustainable use of tropical forests, but in order to assess the back-of-the-envelope guesstimate of existence value, one might look at the developmental uses of tropical forests to see what benefits accrue. If we take Amazonia as an example, the entire GNP of "classical" Amazonia is about 6.4 per cent of Brazil's GNP. In 1980 Brazil's GNP was some $230 billion; thus Amazonia contributed around $15 billion.[12] On the assumption that each adult person in wealthy countries of the world would be willing to contribute $8 per annum to an "Amazon Conservation Fund", the resulting $3.2 billion would enable the people responsible for more than 20 per cent of the economic output of Amazonia to be compensated for ceasing their activities *on the assumption that all existing economic activity is unsustainable*. In practice, Amazon area production of many products – e.g. brazil nuts, latex, fish, crustacea and others – is consistent with the sustainable use of the forest area. Additionally, many services would remain even if much economic activity ceased. Thus, 100 per cent sacrifice of existing development activities is not required.

A closer look at the breakdown of the $15 billion contribution of legal Amazonia to Brazilian GNP in 1980 shows that the broad sectors were: agriculture – $3 billion; industry – $4 billion; services – $8 billion. If we hypothetically assume that all mining and mineral processing was to cease, together with ranching, logging and half the crop production, then the transfer of resources required would be around $5.8 billion in 1980 terms. The outline computations above suggest that 55 per cent ($3.2 billion) of this could be met by international transfers.

These, admittedly, are simplistic calculations. The point is not to estimate exactly the size of existence value but to show that even if we are wrong by a significant amount, there are sizeable economic values for biological diversity conservation. Appropriating those values – i.e. turning them into cash flows for the country in question, and making sure these cash flows compensate the right people – is a further vital issue, and one that will have to be addressed in any biodiversity convention. For the moment, the point of the exercise is to demonstrate that the third feature of the climate problem – high potential economic damage – is as relevant to biodiversity as it is to climate change.

The argument above has been that climate control is not such a major issue as perhaps some of the popular discussions suggest, though it remains a difficult issue. The economic cost burdens are manageable provided policy is addressed in an imaginative way. Biological diversity conservation can also be a fairly low-cost activity, at least initially. Chapter 8 shows that non-timber product revenues may actually *exceed* timber revenues.[13] The implication is that tropical forest conservation might be achieved by a simple appeal to financial profitability. It is likely that much forest is unnecessarily damaged because of a failure to investigate alternative management regimes for alternative "crops". The analysis also raises an important question: if it is *privately* profitable to exploit forests for non-timber products, why isn't greater use made of them for this purpose? In other words, why doesn't the exercise of market forces produce this result?

The answer to this question reveals some of the most important policies for conserving tropical forests. The issue is analysed in detail in Chapter 8, where it is shown that a great deal of deforestation would be avoided if markets were managed to function more efficiently. It is because of direct government interference that the price signals are distorted, making timber extraction – and, more importantly, clearance for agriculture – profitable. The forms taken by this interference are well established and have included, in the case of Brazil:[14]

> tax credits whereby the costs of "investment" in forest land clearance for cattle ranching can be offset against income tax;

subsidized credit for crops and livestock development;
the building of roads which themselves probably would not
pass a benefit-cost test, and which serve to open up areas of
virgin forest to agricultural colonizers.

Equally important in the bias towards clearance is the status of
land tenure. Forest-dwellers frequently have no secure rights
to the land, so that outsiders can readily establish rights
through clearance. Indeed, in many cases, clearance of the
land is a prerequisite for claiming land rights.[15] In the event of
competition for rights, the agricultural colonists invariably win.
Security of land tenure for indigenous peoples may be one of the
most important ways of conserving tropical forests. Conferring
security of tenure on colonists, however, acts like a magnet for
outsiders to clear land for agriculture.

The social irrationality of forest clearance for ranching is
revealed by the fact that, without subsidies, Brazilian beef
cattle ranching revenues probably cover only about one-third
of the costs of setting up the ranches. The subsidy system
explains why what is privately profitable is socially unprofitable.
The combined costs of tax credits, subsidized credit and the
forgone timber revenues from forest destruction in Brazil
is estimated to have been $4.8 billion between 1966 and
1983.

What the analysis reveals is that the world is *needlessly* destroying much of its most precious ecosystems – the rainforests
– and often not in the name of profits for people who need those
profits to survive. If that is right, the policy measures are clear
and, in terms of economic cost, relatively cheap. That does not
make these policies easy to implement, because of the conflict of
interests they generate, but we cannot pretend that conserving
many of the world's ecosystems is expensive. It is not a matter
of expense so much as one of correcting wrong incentives, and
in changing incentives to protect ecosystems we will conserve
biodiversity. It is significant that the Brazilian government has
begun the process of dismantling the financial incentives to
deforest the Amazon: many of the tax allowances have been
removed.

Notes

1. We have explored the economics of "bans" in the context of the African elephant. See E. Barbier, J. Burgess, T. Swanson and D. W. Pearce, *Elephants, Economics and Ivory*, Earthscan, London, 1990.
2. W. Nordhaus, "To Slow or Not to Slow: The Economics of the Greenhouse Effect", Department of Economics, Yale University, mimeo, 1990.
3. See, for example, D. Wirth and D. Lashof, "Beyond Vienna and Montreal – Multilateral Agreements on Greenhouse Gases", *Ambio*, vol. XIX, no. 6–7, October 1990, pp. 305–10; and F. Krause, W. Bach and J. Koomey, *Energy Policy in the Greenhouse*, Earthscan, London, 1990.
4. Krause *et al.*, op. cit.
5. The Stockholm Environment Institute, as reported in the *New Scientist*, 27 October 1990, suggests the 1°C warming limit, a rate of change limit of 0.1°C per decade, and maximum sea level rise (set by limits of adaptation by coral reefs and wetlands) of 2 cm per decade. "Serious threats to human society" occur at rates of 0.2°C per decade.
6. Wirth and Lashof, op. cit.
7. Krause *et al.*, op. cit.
8. Wirth and Lashof, op. cit.
9. "Net" CO_2 emissions are computed according to the World Resources Institute "Greenhouse Index". This imputes global emissions from observed increased atmospheric concentrations of trace gases, and hence allows for any sinks. It then ascribes country-by-country shares of net emissions according to their shares of gross emissions which are observable. See A. Hammond *et al.*, "National Accountability for Global Change: A Comparative Analysis of Greenhouse Gas Emissions", *Environment*, forthcoming, 1991.
10. J. McNeely *et al.*, *Conserving the World's Biological Diversity*, World Bank, Washington, DC, 1990.
11. Some economists express a concern that such valuations may be "counter-preferential", i.e. inconsistent with individuals' preferences in the same way that acts of duty or obligation are counter-preferential. If so, there may be implications for the underlying structure of the welfare economics used to evaluate "resource worth". See D. Brookshire, L. Eubanks and C. Sorg, "Existence Values and Normative Economics: Implications for

Valuing Water Resources", *Water Resources Research*, vol. 22, no. 11, 1986, pp. 1509–18.

12. GNP for Brazil in 1980 was Crz 12281 billion at 1980 prices, and the "legal Amazon" region (Amapa, Para, Roraima, Giais, Acre, Rondonia, Matto Grosso, Amazonas) it was Crz 782 billion. Amazon region's contribution was thus 6.4 per cent in 1980. We have assumed a stable proportion through time. Amazon region's agricultural and ranching GNP was 14.1 per cent of Brazilian agricultural and ranching GNP. We are indebted to Bernadette Gutierrez for the computations.

13. See C. Peters, A. Gentry and R. Mendelsohn, "Valuation of an Amazonian Rainforest", *Nature*, vol. 339, 29 June 1989, pp. 655–6.

14. See D. Mahar, *Government Policies and Deforestation in Brazil's Amazon Region*, World Bank, Washington, DC, 1989; H. Binswanger, *Brazilian Policies That Encourage Deforestation in the Amazon*, Environment Department, World Bank, Working Paper No. 16, Washington, DC, April 1989; R. Repetto and M. Gillis (eds), *Public Policies and the Misuse of Forest Resources*, Cambridge University Press, Cambridge, 1988.

15. See D. Southgate, R. Sierra and L. Brown, *The Causes of Tropical Deforestation in Ecuador: A Statistical Analysis*, London Environmental Economics Centre, LEEC Paper 89–09, 1989.

3

Global Warming: Economics of a Carbon Tax

Scott Barrett

Whenever fossil fuels are burned, carbon dioxide, an important greenhouse gas, is emitted into the atmosphere. Hence users of fossil fuels, however small, contribute to future potential climate change, and the damage associated with such change. Carbon dioxide is only one of many greenhouse gases; others include methane, chlorofluorocarbons (CFCs) and nitrogen oxides. Emissions of all these gases increase atmospheric concentrations of greenhouse gases, and as a general rule one would like to take a comprehensive approach and abate all these pollutants (Stewart, 1990). However, carbon dioxide is particularly important, both because it is emitted in vast quantities and because it persists in the atmosphere for a long time. Any policy intending to reduce atmospheric concentrations of greenhouse gases will therefore have to reduce emissions of carbon dioxide.

In the absence of government intervention, users of fossil fuels will not bear the full costs associated with their actions; these will be borne almost entirely by other people, living in other places and at other times. Hence, we can be sure that emissions will be excessive unless government intervenes. One sensible intervention would be for government to calculate the full damage associated with current use of fossil fuels, and make users of fossil fuels pay for this damage. Users would then seek to avoid having to pay for the damage, and would therefore reduce their emissions.

This proposal for making the polluter pay has many attractions. Economic theory suggests that users would abate emissions as long as the cost of doing so did not exceed the penalty associated with failing to do so – the damage caused by the emissions. In other words, the sum of damages and abatement costs would be minimized. While this is a commendable objective for policy, implementation poses a number of difficulties.

One difficulty is that the potential damage is hard to calculate. An attempt has already been made, and suggests that the figure is between $3 and $107 per ton of carbon (Nordhaus, 1990). However, many people will disagree with these estimates, not least because of the ethical views that lurk behind them. Another difficulty is that each country is likely to care only about the damage *it* would suffer, and ignore the damages its actions impose on other countries. Since abatement by any single country will reduce atmospheric concentrations by a very small amount, this means that countries are unlikely to do much unilaterally. Co-operation is needed. A third problem concerns equity. It seems ethically defensible that the polluter should pay the costs of his or her actions. However, the polluter is not always rich and anonymous and asocial – hence we may want some polluters to pay less than the full damage associated with their actions. We may even want some sufferers to bear a greater share of the burden.

These problems are formidable. However, they plague *any* attempt to manage global climate change, not just proposals for a carbon tax. In fact, the carbon tax might do somewhat better at dealing with these problems than abatement targets. There must certainly be some advantages to a carbon tax. After all, three countries already have one: the Netherlands has a carbon tax of about $1.30, Finland of about $6.10, and Sweden of about $40 per ton.[1]

Prices v. Quantities

Associated with any tax will be a level of abatement. Associated with any level of abatement will be a cost of achieving that abatement at the margin. Saying that we don't know the appropriate tax is the same as saying we don't know the appropriate level of abatement, yet many proposals for abatement levels have been made. The Toronto Conference of 1988 recommended that emissions be reduced 20 per cent from their 1988 level by 2005. The UK government has said that it would stabilize its emissions at the 1990 level by 2005, provided other countries did too. Other EC countries have said that emissions should be stabilized at their 1990 level by 2000 (see Chapter 2). A carbon tax could be employed to achieve these emission targets, and later I shall present estimates of the tax required to meet various targets. However, it is important to recognize that the target could take a different form: the target itself could be a tax.

Which target is most appropriate depends in part on the cost of setting the wrong quantitative target and the wrong tax target. If we impose an emission reduction target, we can be sure about the level of emissions but not the associated cost. If we impose a tax target, we can be sure how much money will be spent to abate emissions at the margin – polluters will spend no more than they would save by not paying the tax – but not the associated emission level.

Although there is some uncertainty about the costs of abatement, there is no doubt that the cost of abating emissions at the margin will rise steeply *eventually*. While there is concern that global warming damages may rise steeply at the margin beyond some threshold, no such threshold has yet been identified. The general circulation models employed to predict the consequences of increased concentrations of greenhouse gases indicate that change is gradual, over both time and space. However, the uncertainties are such that these predictions could be wrong. But since we have no idea *where* such a threshold might exist, let alone *if* such a threshold exists, worry about a threshold would mainly serve to make us undertake greater abatement than we would otherwise undertake. Nevertheless, this greater abatement could be effected by a greater tax. Indeed, the carbon tax can be interpreted as the global warming insurance premium that Mrs Thatcher and others have said we should pay to avoid the potentially harmful consequences of global warming.

A perhaps more compelling reason for preferring the carbon tax target is that abatement will depend not only on the magnitude of the tax but also on the price of fossil fuels, and this price is changeable. If the price of crude oil remains high, it is possible that many countries will achieve the abatement targets mentioned above *without incurring any additional costs* – in other words, no money at all will be spent to avoid potential global warming damages. On the other hand, if oil prices fall back to their earlier levels, the cost of achieving a given quantitative target could turn out to be very high. If we impose a tax, we can be sure that we will always face an incentive to abate emissions, but never too high an incentive. This is one of the great virtues of the carbon tax.

Co-operation

While co-operation is needed if countries are to set a tax that reflects the damages their own use of fossil fuels imposes on others, co-operation is also needed if countries are to choose an emission reduction target that recognizes the damages their emissions impose on others. Whatever the target, co-operation will be needed.

However, the two targets are not identical in their abilities to win agreement by a large number of countries: environmental treaties usually impose identical obligations on different countries. The reason seems to be that it is difficult for countries to come up with an agreed formula for imposing different obligations – partly because the differences will have a great many dimensions. Countries differ in regard to their costs and benefits of abatement, and their ethical views about who should do what. Identical obligations have no rationale other than providing the most obvious answer to the question: "If not here, where?"

An identical abatement obligation will differ from an identical tax. Because abatement costs vary among countries, a uniform abatement obligation will cost some countries much more to meet at the margin than others; and the overall cost of reducing emissions is likely far to exceed that which is necessary to achieve the reductions in total. Indeed, some countries will be made much worse off under such an agreement, and will therefore refuse to co-operate. A nationally administered, uniform tax would involve some countries abating more than others, but it would also ensure that every country paid the same amount of money to abate their last unit of emission, and would hence achieve the total emission reduction at minimum cost. Because the tax would be more efficient, it would probably prove acceptable to a greater number of countries. However, even the uniform tax will make many countries worse off than they would be otherwise, so it will not overcome the problem of winning agreement (Barrett, 1990b).

Equity

Poorer people spend a higher proportion of their total expenditure on energy than higher-income groups, and would therefore bear the greater relative burden of a carbon tax. This is one argument against a carbon tax. However, the argument is flawed for three reasons.

First, given that society wants to do something to reduce greenhouse gas emissions, the relevant comparison is not the well-being of a person or family with and without the tax, but with the tax and some other policy which reduces greenhouse gas emissions. A carbon tax is regressive, but so too are many of the alternatives available for reducing emissions. For example, one suggestion has been for government to establish energy-efficiency standards – minimum levels of energy efficiency for appliances, vehicles, and so on. This may seem to be progressive because owners of these appliances will pay lower energy bills – indeed, the approach has been advocated by the Labour Party in its new environment paper. However, economic research shows that poorer people prefer to buy less energy-efficient goods because of their lower purchase price. A policy of minimum efficiency standards may therefore make poorer people relatively worse off compared with people with higher incomes.

Second, the tax will bring in revenues, and a portion of the revenues can be redistributed to poorer households. What should be contemplated is not simply a tax, but a tax–benefit policy.

Third, the *total* cost of abating emissions can be expected to be lower under a carbon tax. Since every user of fossil fuels would pay the same tax, every user would have the same incentive to reduce emissions. The same would not be true of other policies. For example, if a petrol tax were imposed, car owners would face a greater incentive to abate emissions than other polluters, and the cost of achieving the resulting emission reductions would be excessive. One could always redistribute the efficiency advantages of the carbon tax – the difference between the costs of achieving a given level of abatement by the carbon tax and the alternative policy – to poorer households.

The Carbon Subsidy

When forests are burned, or left to decay, greenhouse gases are released into the atmosphere. But growing forests absorb carbon dioxide, and hence reduce atmospheric concentrations. In reducing atmospheric concentrations, we want not only to reduce emissions but also to enhance absorption. Currently, the temperate forests are in near carbon balance, but the tropical forests are a net source of carbon emissions because huge tracts of these forests are being destroyed with little replanting. We should then seek to slow or halt the rate of tropical deforestation and encourage reforestation, particularly in areas that have been degraded and hence have little alternative use. If a tax is placed on emissions, then a negative tax, or a subsidy, should be placed on forestry activities that enhance the absorption of greenhouse gases. Subsidizing forestry has certain political attractions that are not shared by a tax on fossil fuels.

Setting the Tax

On what basis should the tax be set? Consider first the problem of deciding how the tax should vary by fuel. As noted above, efficiency will demand that the tax be placed on CO_2 emissions and not on fossil fuel use. As Box 3.1 shows, emissions vary with the type of fuel. Coal is more polluting than oil, and oil more than gas. The highest tax should therefore be placed on coal

Box 3.1   **Average CO_2 Emission Coefficients by Fuel**

Fuel	$gC/kBtu^1$	Coal Index
Coal	25.1	1.0
Oil	20.3	0.8
Gas	14.5	0.6

Note: 1. Grams of carbon per thousand Btus.
Source: J. Edmonds and J. Reilly "Global Energy and CO_2 to the Year 2050",
Energy Journal 4, 1983, pp. 21–47.

and the lowest on gas. Non-fossil energy sources, such as hydro and nuclear power, do not emit CO_2, and hence would not be subject to a carbon tax. However, these forms of energy carry their own environmental costs, and as a general rule all prices should reflect environmental and other social costs.

A more difficult issue concerns the absolute magnitude of the tax. How large should the carbon tax be? If the tax is itself the goal of policy, then this question is dual to the one we asked above: By how much should emissions be reduced? As noted above, the answer to this question is not obvious. However, there are advantages to setting a carbon tax and accepting the resulting emission reductions instead of setting a particular emission reduction target. If the tax is simply an instrument for achieving a goal – such as a given level of emission reduction – then the problem of deciding on its absolute magnitude is an analytical one. However, it is still a difficult question to answer, as a substantial body of research is just beginning to show.

The Power of a Carbon Tax

Box 3.2 attempts to summarize the results of some of the research published thus far on the power of a carbon tax – that is, the size of the tax needed to achieve any given level of emission reduction (or, equivalently, the emission reduction associated with any given carbon tax). Extreme care must be

Box 3.2   **Survey of Studies on Carbon Taxes and their Effects**

Source	Carbon Tax ($ per ton)	Oil Price	Percent of Reduction	Emission Region
Nordhaus (1989)	$3	2%[1]	9% in 2050	World
	$37	23%[1]	28% in 2050	
Manne and Richels (1990)	$250 (long run)	158%[1]	75% in 2100 level	World
Cline (1989)	$158[1]	100%	57% in 2050 level or 21% in 1985 level by 2050	World
Edmonds and Reilly (1983)	$123[1]	78%	40% in 2050 level	World
Howarth, Nikitopoulus and Yohe (1989)	$623 (small GDP effect)[9]	103%[8]	26% in 2050 level	World
	$544 (large GDP effect)[9]	103%[8]	47% in 2050 level	
International Energy Agency (1989)	$72[5]	44%[5]	12% in 2005 level	OECD
Bye, Bye and Lorentsen (1989)	$126[1]	75%[6]	20% in 2000 or 0% in 1987 level by 2000	Norway
Barker and Lewney (1990)	$145[1]	92%	18.5% in 2005	UK
	$516[1]	327%	33% in 2005	
Barrett (1990a)[2]	$34[3]	32%[4]	20% in 1988	UK
	$59[3]	57%[4]	20% in 1988 level by 2005	
Ingham and Ulph (1989)	$87–205[1]	57–128%	20% in 1988 level by 2005	UK Manufacturing
Manne and Richels (1989)	$300[7] (long run)	190%[1]	85% in 2100 level or 20% in 1985 level by 2100	USA
Congressional Budget Office (1990)	$28	18%[1]	Stabilize 1990 level through 2000	USA
	$113	72%[1]	10–20% in 1990 level by 2000	

Box 3.2 **Continued**

Notes
1. Assumes that the price of crude oil is $20 per barrel.
2. Revised.
3. Assumes an exchange rate of $1.60 per £.
4. Relative to the 1988 price of imported crude oil, £62 per ton or about £13 per barrel. The second estimate assumes that emissions in 2005 need to be reduced by 35% if the 1988 level of emission is to be reduced by 20%. Ingham and Ulph's (1989) upper-bound estimate assumes that emissions would have to be reduced by almost 50% in 2005 to achieve the same target.
5. The tax is $50 per ton of coal equivalent. The assumed oil price is about $17 per barrel.
6. Bye, Bye and Lorentsen (1989) predict that oil prices would be 5% higher in 2000 if there were no carbon tax. Hence the carbon tax amounts to 75% of the price of oil in 2000, or 80% of the price in 1987.
7. The tax is first applied in 2000 at just over $100 per ton, and reaches a peak of $700 in 2020.
8. The authors apply a 100% tax to a composite of fuels having an average carbon content of 843 KgC per ton of oil equivalent (or 19.8 gC per kBtu). The 103% tax was found by adjusting the 100% tax for the average carbon content of oil (20.3 gC/kBtu). These tax rates are based on prices corresponding to the carbon tax case. Without the carbon tax, the price of energy would be higher – 50% higher when the GDP effect is "small" and 31% higher when the effect is "large" compared to the cases where there is no carbon tax.
9. The price of oil in 2050 is predicted to be $79 per barrel when the GDP effect is "small" and $69 when the effect is "large".
10. Relative to prices in 2050. This is equivalent to a 28% tax on the current price of oil.

taken in interpreting these figures. The table should not be used without reference to the text, because it would be easy to take the results out of context.

In some studies, the tax is reported in $/ton of carbon; in others, as a percentage of the price of fuel in the year in question. To make the results broadly comparable, the size of the tax is presented both in $/ton and on an *ad valorem* basis. In the latter case, the tax is expressed as a percentage of the price of crude oil. Crude oil has the advantage of being an internationally traded commodity. Presenting estimates for oil only, however, can be misleading because the relative magnitude of the tax can vary from study to study. Some of the studies are careful to impose a tax on carbon directly, while others simply impose arbitrary taxes on the different fuels.

These conversions will often not allow direct comparison. For example, the Manne and Richels (1989) estimate of the long-run carbon tax needed to reduce US emissions in 2100 by 20 per cent relative to the 1985 emission level – $300 per ton of carbon – would probably amount to much less than 190 per cent of the price of crude oil in that year, because a century's worth of depletion will probably increase the real price of crude oil substantially above the $20 per barrel price assumed in many of the estimates presented.

The difficulty of determining the power of a tax is complicated even further by volatility in energy markets – for it is the price of the fuels, including the tax, which will determine emissions. The price of a barrel of crude oil increased by more than $10 between August and December 1990 due to the Gulf crisis. A $10 increase in the price of a barrel of crude oil is roughly equivalent to a carbon tax of $77 per ton.

While it is difficult to compare the estimates from one study with those of another, the qualitative story is pretty clear. To lower CO_2 emissions very substantially would require a large carbon tax – larger, certainly, than the taxes already implemented, or for which there exist firm proposals.

Demand-side Responses

The power of a carbon tax – the extent of the emission reduction effected by any given tax – will depend in part on the extent to which the demand for the taxed fuels will change as a result of the tax. The carbon tax can be expected to lead to a substitution of low polluting fuels (natural gas) for more polluting fuels (coal), of non-carbon energy sources (like nuclear) for fossil fuels, and of capital for energy (energy conservation). The full response to the tax will depend on how the tax affects prices, and how prices affect fuel demand. The effect of a change in prices on fossil fuel demand is summarized by the "own-price" and cross-price elasticities for the fossil fuels. These indicate the percentage change in demand for one fuel that would

Box 3.3   Carbon Tax Data

	Base Price[1]	Conversion Factor[2]	Emission Weight[3]
Coal	£35.67/tonne	0.6275	43.2%
Oil	£62.28/tonne	0.8628	37.4%
Gas	21.75 p/therm	0.1450	19.4%

Notes
1. The coal price is the average price of UK coal imports in 1988. The oil price is the average price of UK crude oil imports in 1988. The natural gas price is the average UK price to large industrial consumers in 1988.
2. The coal conversion factor is based on a carbon content of 25.1 gC/kBtu and a heat content of 250 therms/tonne. The oil conversion factor is based on a carbon content of 20.3 gC/kBtu and a heat content of 425 therms/tonne. The gas conversion factor is based on a carbon content of 14.5 gC/kBtu.
3. The weights are for the UK, and are based on estimates of 1988 emissions by fuel supplied by Dr Ken Gregory, British Coal.

Sources: Carbon content from Box 3.1. Prices and heat content from UK Department of Energy (1989).

result from a percentage change in the price of this fuel and closely related fuels, respectively. Unfortunately, there seems to be no consensus about the value of particular energy demand elasticities (see, for example, UK Department of Energy, 1977; Bohi, 1981). This means that the power of a carbon tax could be very uncertain.

Using UK data, Box 3.3 shows how a tax in £/tonne of carbon could be translated into product taxes on the three fuels that emit CO_2: coal, oil, and natural gas. One would simply multiply the carbon tax by the appropriate conversion factor to get an estimate of the product tax corresponding to each fuel. An *ad valorem* tax – which can be interpreted roughly as a percentage increase in the price – could then be computed by dividing the product tax by the base price. If we knew how demand responded to the price increase, we could easily compute the emission reductions associated with any given carbon tax. All we would have to do is calculate the changes in fuel consumption associated with the tax, multiply these changes by the appropriate emission weights, and then sum up the results over all three fuels. As noted above, energy demand elasticities are difficult to estimate with precision. In addition, there is no guarantee that estimates based on history will necessarily do well at predicting future responses. It seems most sensible, then, to see just how important small changes in elasticities can be to the power of a carbon tax.

Estimates of the carbon tax needed to achieve a 20 per cent reduction in UK emissions are shown in Box 3.4. These estimates are computed using the data in Box 3.3 and the given elasticities. These demand elasticities are fairly plausible, but the purpose of the exercise is not to predict the power of a tax but to show how sensitive the tax is to the assumed elasticities. Hence, Box 3.4 is purely illustrative. In interpreting the figures in Box 3.4, note that the "own"-price elasticity of −0.5 for coal implies that a 1 per cent increase in the price of coal (all else being constant) will reduce the demand for that fuel by 0.5 per cent. A "cross"-price elasticity of 0.1 between coal and oil implies that a 1 per cent increase in the price of coal (all else being constant) will increase the demand for oil by 0.1 per cent. Elasticities should be used to predict the response of demand to *small* price changes. However, given the many other factors ignored by this analysis, there is no harm in extrapolating over large price changes – particularly since all we hope to gain is an order-of-magnitude feel for how sensitive the carbon tax might be to different assumptions about the responsiveness of energy demand to the tax.

Three conclusions can be drawn from the analysis summarized in Box 3.4. First, what matters is the entire set of elasticities, not just the own-price elasticities. If both the own- and cross-price elasticities are large, reducing both does not have a big effect on the power of the tax. The intuition behind this conclusion is simple: if it is easy to reduce the use of coal and also easy to move from coal into oil and gas, then the effect of the tax may not be very great; the large reduction in coal emissions will be mitigated by a large increase in oil and gas emissions. Second, a small change in just one elasticity, holding all others constant, can have a big effect on the power of the tax. For example, in comparing rows (5) and (6) we see that increasing the own-price elasticity of coal by −0.5 can change the required carbon tax by a factor of almost three.

Third, different assumptions about the relevant elasticities can deliver very different estimates of the power of a tax. Since the elasticities are uncertain, this means that the power of the

---

Box 3.4 Hypothetical Estimates of the Carbon Tax Needed to Reduce Emissions by 20%

	Elasticity		Carbon Tax			
	Own Price	Cross Price	Carbon (£/tonne)	Coal	Oil	Gas
				(Percent of Base Price)		
(1)	−0.5	0.1	£43	76%	60%	29%
(2)	−0.5, −1 coal	0.1	24	42	33	16
(3)	−0.5	0.2	90	158	125	60
(4)	−0.5, −1 coal	0.2	33	58	46	22
(5)	−1	0.5	£97	171%	134%	65%
(6)	−1, −1.5 coal	0.5	34	60	47	23
(7)	−1	0.25	25	44	35	17
(8)	−1, −1.5 coal	0.25	17	30	24	11
(9)	−1.5	0.75	£65	114%	90%	43%
(10)	−1.5	0.5	22	39	30	15
(11)	−1.5, −2 coal	0.5	16	28	22	11
(12)	−1.5, −1 oil	0.5	31	55	43	21
(13)	−2	0.5	£13	23%	18%	9%
(14)	−2	1	49	86	68	33
(15)	−2	0.75	20	35	28	13
(16)	−2, −1 oil	0.75	40	70	55	27

Source: S. Barrett, *Memorandum* to House of Commons Select Committee on Energy, May 1990.

tax is also uncertain. The power of any given tax is made even more uncertain by the volatility in energy markets. Not only are the demand elasticities subject to uncertainty, but forecasts of the base prices in Box 3.3 are also subject to much uncertainty, as discussed above.

However, we can be sure that where the opportunity for substitution is not great, the carbon tax will prove less powerful. One reason why the tax needed to effect a 20 per cent emission reduction in Norway is so high (see Box 3.2) is that the substitution possibilities are not as great for Norway as they are for other countries. Norway does not burn coal, and has no gas grid. Emissions cannot be reduced by substituting away from coal, and substitution of gas would require costly investment in transmission and distribution (see Bye, Bye and Lorentsen, 1989).

Supply-side Responses

The above sensitivity analysis is for a single country, and assumes that the world prices for energy will not be affected by a unilateral carbon tax. However, if countries comprising a significant proportion of world energy consumption impose a carbon tax, adjustments will take place on the supply side that will serve to erode the power of the tax. Energy suppliers will absorb a part of the tax themselves; the pre-tax price of energy will fall. Hence, in assessing the power of the tax, we will need to know how world energy markets will be affected.

The International Energy Agency (IEA, 1989) predicts that a carbon tax which reduces OECD emissions by 12 per cent in 2005 would reduce consumption of all three fossil fuels. Consumption of coal is expected to fall 28 per cent, petroleum 5 per cent and natural gas 4 per cent in 2005. The IEA (1989, p. 15) predicts that non-OECD emissions will "remain virtually unaffected by the OECD carbon tax". However, we should expect that the tax's effect on energy markets will partially undermine its intent. The tax will lower world demand for fuels with a higher carbon content. World prices for these fuels will fall accordingly, and these lower prices will in turn increase the demand for fuels with a high carbon content – both in the countries that have adopted a carbon tax and, more importantly, in other countries.

Research and Development

Most global warming policy proposals do not look much beyond the beginning of the next century. Targets have been set for emission levels in 2000 and 2005, but few proposals say what level of emission is acceptable in 2006 or 2050 or 2100. Yet atmospheric concentrations will not stabilize unless emissions are prevented from rising. The problem is that any emission ceiling will prove harder to meet over time as economic growth demands greater and greater abatement. Our ability to meet an emission ceiling years from now will depend largely on future developments in technology. The size of the tax needed to achieve any given ceiling in the long run will also depend on future technological innovations.

Manne and Richels (1989) believe that the carbon tax needed to achieve a ceiling in emissions would have to rise substantially over time in order to choke off the demand for fossil fuels. However, once non-carbon-based technologies become available – for example, advanced solar technology – the tax can fall. The very-long-run power of a carbon tax will therefore depend on how large an incentive is needed to bring on the carbon-saving technologies, the timing of such innovations, and their economics. These are even more uncertain than energy demand elasticities.

Revenue-neutral Carbon Tax

A common but bizarre feature of many of the studies cited in Table 3.2 is the usually unstated assumption that the revenue from a carbon tax is lost to the economy. In effect, the carbon tax is assumed to have the same effect as an increase in the price of energy on an economy totally dependent on energy imports. Yet substantial revenues will be generated by the tax, and this money could be put to good use nationally.

Of course, we already have taxes that raise revenues. The problem with these is that most introduce unwelcome distortions into the economy. A tax on income creates disincentives to work: people find it more attractive to substitute untaxed leisure for income-producing activities. Similarly, a tax on investment earnings provides an incentive for consumers to substitute consumption now for consumption later; the rate of savings is depressed. In the United States, such distortions are estimated to impose a total cost of 4-7 per cent of GNP, and a marginal cost of 15–45 cents per extra tax dollar collected (Dower and Repetto, 1990). A carbon tax actually corrects a distortion by making polluters pay for the environmental costs of their actions. Imposition of such a tax would therefore not only help to protect the environment, but also substitute for other revenue sources that damage the economy. At the margin, this substitution could have a significant impact.

Bye, Bye and Lorentsen's (1989) model for Norway offsets the gain in revenue from a carbon tax by reducing the tax on wage income, and increasing transfers to households. Unfortunately, the authors do not show the tax reform's effect on the costs of the emission reductions. However, the offsetting changes in income tax and benefit policy may help to explain why the carbon tax is predicted to reduce GDP in 2000 by only 1 per cent. Barker and Lewney (1990) offset the gains in carbon tax revenues by lowering the Value Added Tax. When the carbon tax is set to reduce emissions 18.5 per cent in 2005, VAT falls to 11.9 per cent (from 15 per cent). When the carbon tax is set to reduce emissions 33 per cent in 2005, VAT falls to 6.7 per cent. As with the Norwegian study, Barker and Lewney (1990) do not calculate the tax offset's effect on the cost of achieving the emission reductions, but they find that the carbon tax has no noticeable effect on GDP growth. Since the carbon tax imposed in this study is quite large, this implies that the efficiency gains from reducing VAT must also be quite large.

Implications for Conventional Pollutants

One consequence of a carbon tax is that it would reduce the emission of conventional pollutants like sulphur dioxide. This is partly because the tax would reduce energy use generally and partly because it would lead to a substitution of cleaner fuels like natural gas for dirtier fuels like coal. This is an additional benefit that should be factored into the cost-benefit calculus of a carbon tax (this benefit is ignored by Nordhaus's [1990] calculation of the optimal tax – see Chapter 2).

Only the study by Bye, Bye and Lorentsen (1989) considers this additional benefit. Concomitant with the 20 per cent CO_2 emission reduction, their model for Norway predicts that emissions of SO_2 would fall by 21 per cent and NO_x by 14 per cent in 2000. If these results were replicated in other countries, the environmental benefit of a carbon tax could be of greater magnitude than estimated by Nordhaus.

It is interesting to point out that this finding is not symmetrical. It is not true that policies to reduce conventional pollutants will necessarily reduce the emission of greenhouse gases. Scrubbing the flue gases of a coal-fired power station could actually increase the emission of CO_2. Natural gas combined cycle conversion, on the other hand, would eliminate SO_2 emissions and reduce NO_x emissions by 90 per cent while reducing CO_2 emissions by two-thirds (American Gas Association, 1989).

Trade

The final complication arises from the global nature of the greenhouse effect, and the difficulty of getting countries to co-operate in managing climate change. If a country imposes a tax unilaterally, then the cost of producing certain domestic goods will rise relative to imports. This means that consumers will substitute imports for domestic output, but production of imported goods will presumably cause more emissions than domestic production because the foreign competition will not have to pay the tax. The environmental consequence of the unilateral tax may therefore be quite small. The offset will be even greater because the tax will lower world energy demand and hence world energy prices. This will provide an incentive for other nations to increase energy consumption and hence emissions. Finally, to the extent that the unilateral action does reduce global emissions, the benefit to any other country of reducing its emissions will probably fall, because the marginal damage caused by these emissions will be lower. This underscores the need for international agreement to be able to control trade with non-signatories, an issue discussed in the next section.

Welfare Implications of Alternative Global Tax Policies

An important consideration in the use of particular instruments is the effect they will have on individual countries. Many of the proposals involve potentially huge distribution effects. From a global efficiency point of view, these distribution effects don't matter, but they will certainly matter to individual countries, and therefore to the negotiating positions of these countries. This means that some proposals will stand a better chance of being adopted internationally than others.

Box 3.5   Welfare Changes for Alternative Emission Reduction Policies

	High-Income	Low-Income	Oil-Exporting	World
	-------(Billions of us Dollars (% GNP))-------			
National	−180	−151	47	−284
Production Tax	(−1.7)	(−4.8)	(10.8)	(−2.0)
National	−67	−121	−108	−269
Consumption Tax	(−0.6)	(−3.8)	(−24.9)	(−2.1)
Globally	−253	94	−123	−282
Administered Tax	(−2.4)	(3.0)	(−28.2)	(−2.0)

Source: J. Whalley and R. Wigle, "Cutting CO_2 Emissions: The Effects of Alternative Policy Approaches", Department of Economics, University of Western Ontario, 1989, mimeo.

Recent work by Whalley and Wigle (1989) provides a sense of how groups of countries will be affected by alternative policies. They consider three policy proposals, and ask how each will affect the welfare (GNP) of three groups of countries: high-income countries with high energy consumption *per capita*, low-income countries with low energy consumption *per capita*, and oil-exporting countries. Each of the proposals is intended to reduce global emissions by 50 per cent in 2005, or 20 per cent of the 1988 level of emission (the Toronto Target). The results of their analysis are summarized in Box 3.5.

If a production tax is placed on fossil fuels by national governments, all countries except the oil exporters will suffer (ignoring the environmental benefits of such a policy). This is because the production tax acts like a rise in the price of fossil fuels; though fossil fuel sales fall, the oil exporters earn substantially more per unit of fuel, and hence come out better. The other countries are all made worse off by this policy. (It should be noted that the tax needed to reduce emissions by 50 per cent in 2005 is estimated to be about 80 per cent of the price of fossil fuels. This is true for all the cases examined.)

If a national consumption tax is placed on fossil fuels, the oil exporters no longer benefit from the tax revenue on production; the effect for them is similar to a fall in world energy demand. Compared with the production tax, oil exporters are made worse off, while both high- and low-income countries are made better off. If a global tax is placed on fossil fuels by an international agency and the tax revenue is redistributed to countries on the basis of their population, the high-income countries are made substantially worse off, while the low-income countries are made better off. The reason is obvious. The high-income countries consume a lot of energy *per capita*, and hence pay a high tax *per capita*. The low-income countries pay a low tax *per capita* because their energy use is relatively low. Since the revenue is redistributed on an equal *per capita* basis, the high-income countries must pay more tax than they receive back, and the low-income countries less tax than they receive back. The effect of this policy would be very similar to a system of tradeable carbon permits where the initial allocation is determined on the basis of population.

It is interesting to point out the scale of the transfers involved in this policy. If the emission reduction is achieved by a national consumption tax, the high-income countries receive $284 billion in national carbon tax revenue. Under the globally administered scheme, these countries would receive just $94 billion in revenue. Hence, the transfer from the high-income countries amounts to about $190 billion (or 1.8 per cent of GNP). In 1986, the OECD countries gave $37 billion in official development assistance, or 0.36 per cent of GNP. This policy therefore demands an unprecedented transfer of wealth.

The insight one gains from this analysis is that the negotiating position of particular countries will depend on the instrument that is used to reduce emissions. Of the three policies considered by Whalley and Wigle, the high-income countries will prefer the national consumption tax, the low-income countries the globally administered tax, and the oil exporters the national production tax. The bargaining range established by this analysis is quite big. Compared with the *status quo ante*, the low-income countries are made substantially better off by the global tax policy, and the oil-exporting countries by the national production tax, even if neither group of countries receives any environmental benefits. The high-income countries are worse off in all three cases, except for the environmental benefits. The challenge for negotiation will be to devise incentives that will make effective agreement possible. The problems these issues pose for negotiating a global warming treaty are discussed in Barrett (1990b).

Notes

1. The Netherlands' tax is intended to raise revenue (about $78 million annually) for public expenditure on environmental protection. Finland's tax is a part of the country's tax reform (see Ad Hoc Committee on Environmental Economics, 1989). Sweden's carbon tax was accompanied by a 50 per cent reduction in energy taxes, and hence will not have the same incentive effect associated with an incremental tax of $40 per ton of carbon. Still, Sweden's carbon tax, combined with other environmental tax changes – including

taxes on the sulphur content of fuels and on emissions of nitrogen oxides – are estimated to reduce CO_2 emissions by 5 to 10 million tonnes by 2000 (National Energy Administration, 1989).

References

Ad Hoc Committee on Environmental Economics (1989), *Economic Instruments for Environmental Protection*, Helsinki: Ministry of the Environment.

American Gas Association (1989), *An Evaluation of Alternative Control Strategies to Remove Sulphur Dioxide, Nitrogen Oxides and Carbon Dioxide at Existing Large Coal-Fired Facilities*, 13 January.

Barker, T. and R. Lewney (1990), "Macroeconomic Modelling of Environmental Policies: the Carbon Tax and Regulation of Water Quality", Department of Applied Economics, University of Cambridge, mimeo.

Barret, S. (1990a), *Memorandum* to House of Commons Select Committee on Energy.

Barrett, S. (1990b), "International Environmental Agreements as Games", paper presented at the Symposium on Conflicts and Co-operation in Managing Environmental Resources, 15–16 November 1990, Siegen, Germany.

Bohi, D. R. (1981), *Analyzing Demand Behaviour: A Study of Energy Elasticities*, Baltimore: Johns Hopkins University Press.

Bye, B., T. Bye and L. Lorentsen (1989), SIMEN: *Studies of Industry, Environment and Energy Towards 2000*, Discussion Paper No. 44, Oslo: Central Bureau of Statistics.

Cline, W. R. (1989), *Political Economy of the Greenhouse Effect*, Institute for International Economics, Washington, DC, August.

Congressional Budget Office (1990), *Reducing the Deficit: Spending and Revenue Options*, Washington, DC: Congressional Budget Office.

Dower, R. and R. Repetto (1990), *Use of the Federal Tax System to Improve the Environment*, prepared for US House of Representatives Committee on Ways and Means Long Term Strategy Hearing on the Environment, Washington, DC, 6 March.

Edmonds, J. and J. Reilly (1983), "Global Energy and CO_2 to the Year 2050", *Energy Journal* No. 4, pp. 21–47.

Howarth, D., P. Nikitopoulus and G. Yohe (1989), "On the Ability of Carbon Taxes to Fend Off Global Warming", Department of Economics, Wesleyan University, mimeo.

Ingham, A. and A. Ulph (1989), *Carbon Taxes and the* UK *Manufacturing Sector*, preliminary draft, Department of Economics, University of Southampton.

International Energy Agency (1989), *Policy Measures and their Impact on CO$_2$ Emissions and Accumulations*, Paris, 7 December.

Manne, A. S. and R. G. Richels (1989), "CO$_2$ Emission Limits: An Economic Analysis for the USA", paper presented at Workshop on Energy and Environmental Modelling and Policy Analysis, MIT Center for Energy Policy Research, 31 July – 1 August.

Manne, A. S. and R. G. Richels (1990), *Global CO$_2$ Emission Reductions: The Impacts of Rising Energy Costs*, Stanford University, February.

National Energy Administration (1989), *Ekonomiska Styrmedel i Miljöpolitiken: Energyi Och Trafik*, Stockholm.

Nordhaus, W. D. (1989), "The Economics of the Greenhouse Effect", Department of Economics, Yale University, mimeo.

Nordhaus, W. D. (1990), "To Slow or Not to Slow: The Economics of the Greenhouse Effect", Department of Economics, Yale University, mimeo.

Stewart, R. B. (1990), "A 'Comprehensive' Approach to Addressing Potential Global Climate Change", discussion paper prepared for the Informal Seminar on US Experience with "Comprehensive" and "Emissions Trading" Approaches to Environmental Policy, Washington, DC, 3 February.

UK Department of Energy (1977), *Report of the Working Group on Energy Demand Elasticities*, Energy Paper No. 17, London: HMSO.

UK Department of Energy (1989), *Digest of United Kingdom Energy Statistics 1989*, London: HMSO.

Whalley, J. and R. Wigle (1989), "Cutting CO$_2$ Emissions: The Effects of Alternative Policy Approaches", Department of Economics, University of Western Ontario, mimeo.

4

Global Warming:
The Economics of Tradeable Permits

Anil Markandya

Introduction

In the previous chapter, we discussed the use of national and international taxes as a means of controlling atmospheric trace gases (ATGS), the principal one of which is carbon dioxide. One can think of such a tax as a "price" for the right to emit ATGS into a global environmental sink. Once the price is fixed, emissions are adjusted and the task before the regulatory authority is to set the right tax, or price, so that the desired level of emissions is obtained. However, the problem can be approached in another way. The regulators could specify the emissions reductions, and then allow the market mechanism to determine the price. It would work through the issuance of ATG permits, which would be traded, perhaps on some kind of exchange, and from which a price would emerge. This price would be the equivalent of a tax.

In a simple model, with the demand for permits – or equivalently the costs of reducing ATGS – known with certainty, the two approaches should result in the same outcome.

This can be seen with the aid of a diagram (Box 4.1 below). On the vertical axis are the additional (or marginal) costs of reducing emissions in two different countries: a rich developed country and a poor developing country. The rich country has a higher level of emissions to start with but a lower marginal cost of reducing emissions than the developing country. If we combine the two marginal reduction costs, we obtain the overall marginal cost curve for reductions in emissions. Note that total emissions (OB) are the sum of the individual emissions (OF for the poor country plus OC for the rich country). If we

Box 4.1

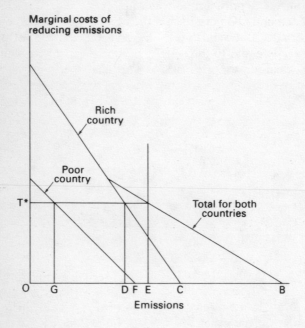

want to reduce emissions from OB to OE, a tax of T* should be imposed. With this tax the poor country would cut back emissions from OF to OG, and the rich country would cut back from OC to OD. The reason for each country cutting back by precisely that amount is that it equates the tax to the marginal cost of reduction. Any further cutbacks would imply a cost of reduction greater than the tax payment saved, and a cutback less than that would imply a unit tax payment greater than the cost of a unit reduction. The sum of FG and CD is equal to BE. Note also that with a tax of T* the revenue collected from the poor country would be OGxT* and from the rich country, ODxT*. The two together amount to OExT*.

With a permit system, the regulatory authority would issue a total number of permits equal to OE. Each country's demand for permits is now given by its marginal costs of abatement function. At a price for the permits of T* the poor country would demand OG permits and the rich country would demand OD permits. Between them, the total demand for permits is then exactly equal to the supply and the market for permits is exactly cleared at a price of T*. Note that the total payments for the permits are exactly the same as the payment of taxes: OGxT* by the poor country and ODxT* by the rich country.

If the two methods of control have the same solution, why then do some economists argue in favour of one rather than the other? The reasons lie in the impact of uncertainty on the solutions and in the details under which the two systems operate.

Taxes and Permits: The Impact of Uncertainty

The central assumption made so far, which is clearly violated, is that these reduction cost curves are known with certainty. They are not, and there is considerable argument about what the costs of reducing ATGS are. In the presence of uncertainty, a tax may result in a *level* of reduction that is different from the desired reduction; on the other hand, a permit system could result in a *cost* of reduction on the participants that is different from the anticipated cost. Both types of error have adverse implications. If a change results in too low a reduction in emissions, the effect in terms of global climate change could be serious. On the other hand, an issue of permits that is too small could result in very high costs of reduction, in terms of forgone growth of output and a decline in living standards.

As a matter of common sense, economists argue that one should go for price-based controls when the potential losses from incorrectly estimating costs are relatively large, and for quantity-based controls when the potential losses from achieving the emissions reductions targets are relatively large. In the case of global climate change, it is hard to say which of the two costs are greater. However, in the case of permits, there is scope for mitigating any unforeseen high cost of reduction by adjusting the allocation of permits, or recycling the revenues collected by the sale of permits in an appropriate manner. With the tax solution, one cannot adjust the emissions reductions effects in the same way, although one could adjust taxes in future periods if the observed rates of emissions reduction was too low or too high. As long as taxes are flexible, this would be an acceptable solution, but the setting and changing of international taxes may prove too difficult to implement and therefore not amenable to the kinds of adjustments that are required. Also, it should be noted that where taxes have been employed as environmental control instruments in other contexts, the level of changes has consistently tended to be too low (Opschoor and Voss, 1989).

Setting the Target

With a permit system, one of the key tasks is to define the target level of reductions. For ATGs the targets being discussed are almost entirely in terms of carbon dioxide emissions. For example, the Toronto Target, set in 1989 by a group of concerned citizens, called for a 20 per cent reduction in CO_2 emissions from 1988 levels by 2005. More recently, discussion has focused on a target of stabilizing global CO_2 emissions at 1990 levels by 2005. This latter target (which is consistent with the Nordwijk Declaration of 1990 made by the Environment Ministers of several countries) is based on an "ecological sensitivity value", whereby an ecologically tolerable rate of global warming is thought to be about 0.1°C per decade. To limit warming to this level, one would need to phase out CFCs and to reduce CO_2 emissions by around 20 per cent compared to the projected 2005 levels.

The choice of a target based on such an "ecological sensitivity" criterion turns out to be considerably stricter than one that would appear to emerge from a comparison of costs and benefits of global warming. A detailed worldwide analysis of the damages arising from global warming has not been carried out, but it is interesting to note that on the basis of the evidence from a preliminary US-based study, extrapolated to all countries, a lower emissions target would be indicated (Nordhaus, 1990; Ayres and Walter, 1990).

The other aspect of the targets for reductions is the fact that only CO_2 emissions are considered; these account for only half of all ATGS. This is mainly because CO_2 emissions are more readily monitored than other ATGS (apart from CFCS). The latter are being dealt with through the Montreal Protocol, and the feeling is that politically it is easier to negotiate agreements in a gas by gas bans. From an efficiency point of view, however, such a procedure could involve considerably higher costs. It might be cheaper to allow some countries to reduce other ATGS, or to exploit their carbon sink capacities, rather than cut back on carbon emissions. This possibility is not allowed for.

Allocating the Permits

How would a permit system work in practice? A central authority could act as an auctioneer and, using a bidding process (open or closed), would allocate CO_2 permits for fixed periods of time. Bids would be made by governments, on the basis of what they felt the demand for emissions in their respective countries would be. However, we have no experience with such an auction applying in this context, and for what would be such large sums of money. Just to get an idea of what would be involved: emissions of CO_2 worldwide in 1987 were around 19 million metric tons, or around 5 billion tons of carbon. If a permit price of £20–30 per ton of carbon were to emerge – a plausible range, according to some estimates (Grubb, 1990) – the revenue raised would be in the range of $100–150 billion! Any authority controlling such sums would be very powerful, probably too powerful for governments to be willing to give it a mandate.

The alternative solution is to allocate permits to countries on the basis of existing emissions, or on some other criterion. Trading would then take place between countries, with those whose costs of reducing emissions are lower than the average selling permits, and those with relatively high emissions reduction costs buying permits. An exchange or clearing house would be useful, but not essential, and the financial transfers involved would be smaller than in an open auction. The *key* issue here, of course, is how the initial allocation is made. In other applications of permit systems (McGartland and Oates, 1985); (Tietenburg, 1990) the commonest method is to allocate permits in proportion to current use. This criterion, known as grandfathering, would result in the largest number of permits being given to the developed countries (46 per cent) and Eastern Europe (28 per cent); and the minority going to developing countries (26 per cent). Given the higher aspirations for economic growth in the developing world, such an allocation would be considered extremely inequitable. More importantly, developing countries would never accept a system based on such an allocation. Much the same applies to an allocation based on GDP – i.e. each country receives permits in proportion to its share of the world's GDP.

A seemingly just way to allocate tradeable permits would be on the basis of population. After all, if the global environment is a truly public good, each of us has an equal share in it. On that basis, however, the giant nations of India and China would get the lion's share and the rich countries would have to purchase back a lot of permits at a significant cost. Some have argued that such a transfer from the rich to the poor is warranted anyway, and it would be a good way of enforcing the transfer of resources from the North to the South. However, such a view fails to realize that an agreement on global warming has to be based on a broad consensus, with each country finding the terms acceptable. A population-based allocation of permits would not command such a consensus, any more than a GDP- or grandfathering-based one.

Considerable thought has been given to alternative rules for allocating permits that are both "fair" and acceptable. For the GDP-based allocation system, it has been argued that account should be taken of the fact that exchange rates do not reflect purchasing power, and that a country's allocation should be based on its "true" as opposed to its dollar-value GDP. Another adjustment that has been proposed is to allocate permits on the basis of adult populations, rather than total populations.

The argument here is that a total-population rule may encourage population growth, or at least reduce the incentives for population control, in the interests of getting more permits. Incidentally, since the fast-growing populations of developing countries tend also to have a larger non-adult share, this rule redresses some of the advantage given to those countries by the population rule.

The essential problem remains, however, that whatever rule is to be used has to command *universal* acceptability. Developing countries, with projected economic growth rates of 5 per cent per annum and more, are simply unwilling to agree to any measures that would involve more than a marginal reduction in that rate of growth. Hence, the allocation of permits has to be sufficient for them to be able to pursue their growth targets. If that is to be the case, the developed countries will have to cut back their emissions by even more. Conflict could also arise from the way in which permits are allocated on the grounds of inequity of previous cutbacks. For example, a country such as France has very low emissions of CO_2 because it has pursued a programme of nuclear power generation. If the rule for allocating permits did not recognize that, it would face a much higher cost of meeting the global target than a country which had not pursued such a programme. Finally, there are other considerations of "need". What about countries, such as Canada and Finland, where energy needs are high because of the climate? Or countries such as Australia, where much of the indigenous fuel (coal) has a high carbon content?

For all these reasons, it is unlikely that a global sharing of permits can *ever* be agreed. What is possible, however, is for groups of countries in similar positions to agree *targets*. If such targets are undershot, or likely to be overshot, these countries may also agree to some informal arrangement for trading their respective surpluses or deficits. In fact this was the way permit trading in the environmental sphere arose in the first place, and much the same could happen with regard to CO_2 emissions.

Experience with Permit Trading

Experience with permit trading in general is mixed. Under the bubble concept in the United States, firms that had over-achieved their Clean Air Act targets could transfer their surplus reductions to other firms. In fact much of the trading that took place under this arrangement was intra-corporation, and the overall market for genuine trades was quite thin (thought to number only a few hundred). However, there may be special reasons why permit trading was a failure in this context. Hahn (1989) argues that it was partly the result of the administrators being unwilling to encourage such trades, because of the criticisms of environmentalists. The latter have been against such trading on the grounds that it conferred the "right to pollute". In the context of permits for CO_2, such objections might be less severe.

On economic grounds, the evidence in favour of trading is quite strong. Tietenberg (1990) has shown that such schemes could cost anything between five and ten times less than schemes involving direct regulations. If this were to hold for CO_2, the savings worldwide would be enormous. For example, if emissions were to be reduced by 20 per cent over current levels, the reduction would be around one billion tons of carbon. Assuming an efficient cost of £20–30 per ton (see above), the total cost would be in the region of £20–30 billion. An inefficient system costing five times as much would cost £100–150 billion! Hence if these cost savings could be achieved, there would a strong case for a permit trading system.

Another difficulty that has emerged from the trading experience with permits is the tendency of the more powerful traders to hoard them. Given uncertainties regarding the future availability of permits, and the desire to gain monopoly power, traders have responded in a number of cases by hoarding. The same could happen with permits for greenhouse gases, if rich countries buy up permits to keep poor countries from producing goods that would compete with their own in the international markets.

Finally, Tietenberg has argued that permit systems in the

United States have encouraged technological progress in pollution control. This is particularly true in the case of the substitution of water-based solvents for solvents using volatile organic compounds (vocs). The reason is simply that with permit trading there is a continuous incentive for purchasers to find ways of reducing their demands for permits.

Conclusions for the Use of Permits to Control Greenhouse Gas Emissions

What are the implications of the experience in permit trading for the control of greenhouse gas emissions? The arguments in favour are the clear economic benefits that could be derived, and the encouragement that the system offers for continued technological developments that limit emissions through increased energy efficiency. On the negative side are the difficulties with actual trading arrangements, and the possibility of countries hoarding permits and using monopoly power to eliminate competition. What must also be borne in mind is the fact that any agreed trading system would work only if the countries party to such an agreement were to *continue* to be satisfied that the system worked. This acts as a positive force in so far as it discourages hoarding and other destabilizing behaviour, but it also acts as a negative force because it would need only a few bad experiences with the system for it to collapse and the whole arrangement to fail.

Given all these objections – and in view of the difficulties with allocating permits in the first place – it is very unlikely that a full permit system can be instituted for greenhouse gases in the foreseeable future. What could happen, however, is that limited trades take place, based on targets for reductions in emissions that are partly regional and partly based on the level of development. Such trading is not to be sniffed at; it can generate considerable benefits and may, in time, be the precursor to a global trading arrangement. As an alternative to a global carbon tax, it certainly deserves serious consideration.

References

Ayres, R. and J. Walter (1990), "Global Warming: Abatement Policies and Costs", International Institute of Applied Systems Analysis, Laxenberg, Austria, mimeo.

Grubb, M. (1990), *The Greenhouse Effect: Negotiating Targets*, London: Royal Institute of International Affairs.

Hahn, R. (1989), "Economic Prescriptions for Environmental Problems: How the Patient Followed the Doctor's Orders", *Journal of Economic Perspectives*, vol. 3, no. 2, pp. 95–114.

McGartland, A. and W. Oates (1985), "Marketable Permits for the Prevention of Environmental Deterioration", *Journal of Environmental Economics and Management*, vol. 12, pp. 207–28.

Nordhaus, W. (1990), "To Slow or Not to Slow: The Economics of the Greenhouse Effect", Department of Economics, Yale University, mimeo.

Opschoor, J.B. and H.B. Voss (1989), *Application of Economic Instruments for Environmental Protection in OECD Countries*, Paris: OECD.

Tietenberg, T. (1990), "Economic Instruments for Environmental Regulation", *Oxford Review of Economic Policy*, vol. 6, no. 1, pp. 17–33.

5

Economics and the Ozone Layer

Anil Markandya

Chlorofluorocarbons – or CFCs, as they are called – are organic compounds that have been widely used for over three decades in air conditioners, refrigerants, aerosols, foams (as blowing agents), solvents and sterilants. Manufacture began on a large scale in the early 1960s. It was only in the 1970s, however, that suspicions began to be raised about a possible link between the use of these products and related compounds called halons (used in fire-extinguishing equipment) and damage to the stratospheric ozone layer. Evidence on this link mounted over a number of years, throughout the 1980s, until there is now almost unanimous consensus about it.

Scientific evidence on the damage to the ozone layer has been accompanied by studies, largely in the USA, on the impact of this damage to health and materials. Again there is substantial agreement that the use of CFCs and halons has led, via this route, to an increased incidence of skin melanomas, cataracts and related diseases. Furthermore, through its increased concentrations of ozone in the tropospheric ozone layer, it has been implicated in damage to agriculture (particularly to crops such as soya beans), aquatic life and building materials, and health effects associated with smog. More recently, as research on the causes of global warming has advanced, it has also been found that CFCs are significant contributors to global warming. Details of greenhouse gases are given in Chapter 3, but broad figures indicate that the warming potential of CFCs is between 1500 and 7300 times that of carbon dioxide on an equivalent weight basis. In total terms, CFCs account for around 10 per cent of the warming impact over a hundred-year period.

Pressure for some reduction in the use of CFCs began to grow in the early 1980s. At that time there were no studies showing how the damage attributable to these chemicals compared to the costs of limiting their use. In 1987, the United States Environmental Protection Agency (USEPA, 1987a) published the findings of a study showing that the benefits of control were *far* higher than the costs – by a factor of over 150 in most scenarios. Benefits were estimated using costs of avoided treatment, and values of lives saved, as well as results from models that looked at the relationship between ozone concentrations and agricultural yields. The costs were largely based on the assumed costs of replacing CFCs by more expensive substances that did not have an ozone-depleting potential (or had a much smaller one). Box 5.1 below summarizes the results of that study. Although there is some scepticism among policy-makers about the use of cost-benefit analysis for evaluating regulations on environmental problems,[1] the sheer magnitude of the difference between benefits and costs in this area meant that the evidence could not be ignored. At the same time, manufacturers such as Dupont in the United States and ICI in the United Kingdom, anticipating some regulatory control, had begun to invest in research in alternatives. Their research

---

Box 5.1   **Benefits and Costs for the USA of controlling CFCs**

| | | *($ billion)* | | |
Level of Control	*Benefits*	*Costs*	*Net Benefits*	*Net Incremental Benefits*
Freeze	3314	7	3307	3307
20% Cut	3396	12	3384	77
50% Cut	3488	13	3475	31
80% Cut	3533	22	3531	56

All figures are discounted present values, covering the period 1987–2075. Cuts are assumed to apply from 1986 levels.

Source: USEPA, *Regulatory Impact Analysis of Stratospheric Ozone*, vols I–III, Washington, DC: Environmental Protection Agency, 1987.

---

showed that substitutes could be produced at a reasonable cost. The fact that they would have a head start in the field made them willing partners in any control process.

That process was carried out largely by the United Nations Environment Programme (UNEP). It was the obvious body to carry out this work, as the problem is one of a global nature. The ozone layer is the same for everyone, and a ton of CFC has the same impact irrespective of where in the world it is used. As the products using CFCs are relatively sophisticated, it is not surprising that the richer, developed countries were (and are) producing more CFCs than the developing countries. Box 5.2 below gives details of consumption of CFCs and halons by country in 1986 and, *assuming no controls*, in the year 2000. Because of the faster growth in demand for products such as aerosols and refrigerators in developing countries, their share of the total would rise from 15 per cent in 1986 to 22 per cent in 2000, and even further thereafter. Thus, although it was not critical to get the agreement of the developing countries at the early stages, it would become increasingly so in the future.

Box 5.2   **Uses of CFCs and Halons by Region**

(000 tonnes)

	1986		2000	
	Total	*%*	*Total*	*%*
North America	370	30	583	27
Other Developed Countries	493	40	777	36
USSR & E. Europe	185	15	346	16
All Developing Countries	180	15	479	22
Total	1228	100	2185	100

Source: United Nations Environment Programme, *Economic Panel Report* (1989) and author's calculations.

The Montreal Protocol

The Montreal Protocol was signed in 1987. The thirty-six signatories, who accounted for over 80 per cent of total consumption, agreed to reduce their consumption of the five major chlorofluorocarbons and three important halons with effect from January 1989. The reduction was to have been 50 per cent of the July 1986 level by 1998, but this was raised to 85 per cent in a subsequent follow-up agreement (the Helsinki Agreement) in 1988. These terms applied to "developed countries" – defined as those with a *per capita* consumption of CFCs of over 0.3 kg. For countries with a lower level of consumption, a grace period of ten years was agreed, so that they would have to phase down consumption to 15 per cent of their 1986 levels by 2008. Each country was to achieve its target as it thought best. This meant that those that favoured market-based instruments could use them, and those that preferred the more command-and-control policies could apply those. From an economist's point of view, such agreements, where the reductions are more or less *pro rata*, are generally viewed as inefficient. This is because some countries can cut production back more easily than others, and it would be desirable for those who can cut back at lower cost to bear a larger share of the cuts.[2] If the ensuing division of the burden is deemed to be unfair – or, more importantly, *unacceptable* – some form of transfer of resources will have to be made so that all parties view the situation after the cuts as preferable to the one before them.

Efficiency and Consensus

Efficiency arises at two levels in connection with agreements such as these. The first is the allocation of cuts between countries; the second is the way in which cuts are achieved within each country. In connection with the Montreal Protocol, the latter is at least as important as the former. The technological options and costs for shifting from CFCs to the substitutes are pretty much internationally determined. They vary from product to product, with the costs of substituting for CFCs in mobile air conditioning and domestic refrigeration being the highest. This would suggest that countries in which these uses of CFCs were the most dominant would face higher substitution costs. North and Latin America, and the Near and Middle East, are areas where this is the case. However, as substitution takes place, prices are expected to fall rapidly. If the substitution of the more expensive items can be delayed towards the end of the period, this impact should not be too great. On the other hand, the scope for cost efficiency or inefficiency within a country are substantial.

This can be seen through the following example. Domestic refrigeration and mobile air conditioning are major users of CFCs, and at present the costs of substitution are very high relative to other uses. Box 5.3 gives some indication of likely costs of substitutes in individual sectors, along with dates at which they are estimated to be available. If a government demands substitution of all materials in all uses on the same basis – e.g. 12 per cent reduction per annum to achieve the 85 per cent reduction by 1998 – the costs could be very high. If, however, it introduces a progressive tax on users, the substitution will take place on a cost-efficient basis, with the cheapest sources substituting out of CFCs first. True, the users of CFCs in

---

Box 5.3   Costs of CFC Substitutes and Dates of Availability

	Additional Cost	Available Dates
Aerosols	Nil	Available Now
Industrial Refrigerants	0.95	1995
Solvents	1.15	1993
Non-Rigid Foam Blowing	1.75–›0.8	1990–1998
Rigid Foam Blowing	1.75–›0.8	1990–1998
Comfort Air Conditioning	1.45–›0.95	1990–1998
Domestic Refrigeration	14.60–›11.90	1995–1998
Mobile Air Conditioning	13.25–›10.95	1994–1998

Note: Where more than one figure is given, the cost is expected to fall from the higher to the lower figure over the time interval given in the second column.
Source: McKinsey & Co., Protecting the Global Environment: Funding Mechanisms (Noordwijk, November 1989).

---

products such as refrigerators and air conditioners will have to pay a charge, but the amounts are unlikely to have a major impact on the industries in terms of output and employment, and the proceeds can be used to assist those manufacturers who may face difficulties in adapting their technology to the newer products. A charge would also provide an incentive to recycle existing CFCS. The technology for doing so exists for some products, but will develop as it responds to the incentives of a price differential between new and recycled CFCS.

The conclusion from this discussion is that efficiency is an issue with regard to the Montreal Protocol, but it arises more from how the targets are met internally than from how they are allocated across countries. The latter can then be addressed more explicitly as a question of consensus, which requires that all parties find the situation preferable *ex post*, otherwise they will not sign the agreement and there is no way they can be forced to do so. The task of the co-ordinating agency is to find an allocation of cuts, and a set of transfers between countries, such that all of them want to be party to the Protocol. In the simplest model of searching for such bargains, each country is deemed to weigh its own costs and benefits inside and outside the agreement, and then to decide whether or not to join. However, if such models of self-interest really applied, the world would be in trouble. This is because *any* medium-to-small country can always obtain the benefits of a protocol without joining it. Its own emissions of CFCS are likely to make a negligible impact on the damage it suffers, but it will face a cost if it joins. In economic terminology it can play the role of a "free rider" in the agreement. If every country did this, however, there would be no agreement.

Fortunately, this is not the way countries have responded. Most have accepted that the protection of the ozone layer is desirable and that all nations will have to contribute to that protection by reducing their use of CFCS. Rather, the question that has been posed is one of equity. The developing countries have argued that they need some assistance with the change in technology, so that living standards are not jeopardized as a result of having to shift to the new products. Thus the "individualist-rationalist" model does not seem to apply, but rather one based on co-operation and burden-sharing.[3] Unfortunately, this is not an area where traditional bargaining models are of much help.

Sharing the Burden

It has long been an accepted part of the negotiations undertaken to reduce emissions of CFCs and halons that developing countries should have some assistance with meeting the terms of any agreed phasing out of these substances. As stated earlier, the original Montreal Protocol included a concession to developing countries in the form of a ten-year grace period in which the reductions to 15 per cent of the 1986 level were to be achieved. In addition, the consumption and production targets for these countries were also more lax, and they were permitted more flexible arrangements to trade controlled substances than developed countries.

Such concessions were not considered enough by many of the developing countries (including India and China) who argued that they needed more assistance with the industrial restructuring and transfer of technology involved if they were to be able to afford the transition. The Montreal Protocol – under Article 5, which dealt with the special situation of developing countries – had committed parties to "facilitating access to environmentally safe alternative substances and technology" and to "facilitating bilaterally or multilaterally the provision of subsidies, aid credits, guarantees or insurance programmes" for the use of substitute products.

As the first step in creating a mechanism for such assistance, it was necessary to estimate the needs of the developing countries to meet the terms of the Protocol as it applied to them. One such study, carried out by the author (Metroeconomica, 1989) found that for short-term assistance with industrial restructuring, a figure of around $200 million for the first three years would be required. This figure was supported by an independent study carried out by the USEPA (1990). On the basis of a sector-by-sector analysis, the study concluded that the total costs for the first three years would be between $162 and $262 million. Both these studies influenced the agreement reached in London in June 1990, when an interim Multilateral Fund of $160 million was set up, which would be raised to $240 million if India, China and other non-signatories were to become parties to the Protocol. The latter now looks very likely, at least as far as the first two countries are concerned.

In the longer term, assistance will also be needed to meet the higher costs of CFC substitutes. Estimating this is difficult, given that many of the substitutes are not even available in developed countries on a commercial basis. However, given estimates of expected market prices, and their fall over time as economies of scale came into operation, a figure of around $1.8 billion over the period 1990–2008 was arrived at in the Metroeconomica Study. This was a discounted present value based on a 5 per cent real discount rate and was considered, if anything, on the high side. Since then a number of country studies of the costs of meeting the terms of the Montreal Protocol have been commissioned and a few have been completed, including studies on China, Egypt, India and Mexico. It is difficult to compare the results of these studies, and to obtain an overall estimate, but from an initial examination of the data it appears that:

(a) the costs will probably be "bunched", with not much being incurred between 1994 and 1998 but a substantial amount being incurred between 1998 and 2010;
(b) there are big differnces between the figures for the medium-sized countries, such as Egypt and Mexico, and the large ones, such as India. These differences cannot be resolved until more country studies have been done and the methodology has been properly reviewed within a consistent framework;
(c) the costs of meeting a given target can be large or small, depending on how efficient the process of transfer is. Apart from the Indian study, this question has not really been addressed.

Thus it is not possible to say with any certainty what the fund required after 1994 will be. Preliminary indications are that it will not be large for the first few years after that. The Metroeconomica estimate of around $1.8 billion at a 5 per cent discount rate is probably as good as any. However, the issue of efficiency *is* important. In particular, the way in which the resources are transferred could influence that. The following two examples will show why.

First, there is the issue of whether a country should manufacture CFC substitutes, or import them. In some cases, existing plant for CFC 11 and CFC 12 can be switched to the production of less ozone-depleting substances such as HCFC 22, and only the cost of switching needs to be allowed for. In other cases, new manufacturing facilities will have to be installed, or the more expensive material will have to be imported. If one takes the approach that local manufacturing facilities would have to be set up as soon as was practicable, even if this was not economically efficient compared to importing the substances, then the costs of substitution are certain to be higher. That was the assumption made in the Indian study, where a fee was included for the transfer of technology to the companies responsible for developing the substitutes. Even assuming such a deal could be struck with the large Western chemical companies (which is not clear), from an efficiency point of view such a procedure is bound to come up with a higher cost of compliance than one based on importing new products as needed until domestic production on a competitive basis can be set up. Experience with CFC 11 and CFC 12 would suggest that the costs of production for substitutes such as HCFC 123 and HCFC 134a will fall rapidly as production increases worldwide. Small producers such as India can then purchase the technology at a reasonable rate, rather than attempting to enter production at the earliest possible opportunity.

The second example relates to efficiency in substitution, and again the Indian study is a good example. Data on that country reveal that domestic refrigerators have a very long effective life. If CFCs are made unavailable from 2006 or thereabouts, a large number of them will have to be replaced suddenly, entailing a large cost. The way to avoid this, of course, is to have a stock of CFCs and a recycling facility that keeps substances available for the effective life of the equipment that needs them. In the first phase of the Indian study no account was taken of this possibility, and the substitution costs for the country came out very high. In some subsequent analysis, however, recycling was allowed for, and its costs were built into the analysis. The revised figures were then very much lower, by an order of magnitude. Thus a programme of assistance that did not allow for or did not encourage such recycling could be much more expensive than one that did.

Conclusions on the Montreal Protocol

The story of the Montreal Protocol and the control of the use of CFCs is both encouraging and instructive. It is encouraging because it represents a case where nation-states with very diverse starting points got together and agreed to the virtual phase-out of environmentally damaging substances. This involved complex negotiations, and transfers to developing countries, but the difficulties were resolved, a facility for making the transfers was put into place and a broad agreement was arrived at. It is instructive because the relevant model of bargaining was not a simple individualist/conflict-based one, but rather one based on co-operation and notions of justice. An appreciation of the universality of the problem and the need to resolve it shone through the complexities and details of some very hard-headed negotiations.

At the same time, it is important to note that this is not a good indicator of what difficulties will be faced in negotiations with other environmental problems. There are a number of explanations for the fact that this Protocol was successful, while others may not be so easy to achieve. One is that the transfers required were, relatively speaking, small. The developed countries could afford to make the payments into the fund and justify them to themselves on the grounds of their own benefits. The second is that the costs of an agreement of equi-proportional cuts were not too high. The nature of the technology for substitution and its openness mean that an agreement whereby everyone phased out use did not place a unequally large burden on some countries relative to others. The process of phasing out CFCs had in fact started several years earlier, when the producers of these chemicals started to carry out research on alternatives.

Unfortunately, neither of these conditions holds for the problems of global warming or biodiversity. The transfers required here *are* certain to be much larger, and the costs of simple agreements such as those of the Montreal Protocol to be unacceptably high.

Notes

1. See, for example, USEPA (1987b). This study provides a mixed assessment as far as the use of cost-benefit analysis in regulation is concerned. For a more positive assessment, see J. P. Barde and D. W. Pearce (eds), *Valuing the Environment*, Earthscan, 1991.
2. The rule for efficiency is that the cuts in production should be such that the cost of an additional reduction should be the same wherever it is made. For example, if the United States could cut consumption by 1000 kg at a cost of $5000, and the United Kingdom at a cost of $10,000, then it would reduce overall costs by $5000 if the USA cut its output by a further 1000kg and the UK *increased* its output by the same amount.
3. For an example of the application of the more individualist models of bargaining in the area of international agreements, see Barrett (1989).

References

Barde, J. P. and D. W. Pearce (eds), (1991), *Valuing the Environment*, London: Earthscan.

Barrett, S. (1989), *On the Nature and Significance of International Environmental Agreements*, London: London Business School, mimeo.

McKinsey & Co. (1989), *Protecting the Global Atmosphere: Funding Mechanisms, Second Report to the Ministerial Conference on Atmospheric Pollution and Climate Change*, The Hague.

Metroeconomica (1989), *The Costs to Developing Countries of Joining the Montreal Protocol*, Nairobi, Kenya: United Nations Environment Programme, OzL.Fin.1.

USEPA (1987a), *Regulatory Impact Analysis of Stratospheric Ozone*, vols I–III, Washington, DC: Environmental Protection Agency.

USEPA (1987b), EPA's *Use of Benefit Cost Analysis 1981–1986*, Washington, DC: Environmental Protection Agency.

USEPA (1990), *Preliminary Analysis of Capital Costs for CFC Reductions for the First Three Years*, Washington, DC: Environmental Protection Agency.

United Nations Environment Programme (1989), *Economic Panel Report, Pursuant to Article 6 of the Montreal Protocol*, vol. 3, Nairobi: Kenya.

6

Environmental Degradation in the Third World

Ed Barbier

The view that environmental conservation "matters" for sustainable development in the poor world received its most popular exposition in the highly influential Brundtland Report, in 1987 (World Commission on Environment and Development, 1987). The Commission stated:

> Failures to manage the environment and sustain development threaten to overwhelm all countries. Environment and development are not separate challenges; they are inexorably linked. Development cannot subsist upon a deteriorating environmental resource base; the environment cannot be protected when growth leaves out of account the costs of environmental destruction. (p. 37)

The influence of the Brundtland Report was not simply a result of its timely reiteration of the "sustainable development" theme. An important departure of the Report from previous statements on this theme was the explicit recognition of the role of economics in both analysing the *costs of environmental degradation* in the Third World and in designing appropriate *incentives* for its alleviation.

Economic and Ecological Linkages

All definitions of environmental degradation suggest that it is a complex process resulting from human exploitation of ecological resources and functions (see Box 6.1). For environmental degradation to be an *economic problem*, however, requires it to have a *cost* in terms of a loss of human welfare, either directly

Box 6.1   Environmental Degradation – Some Definitions

Simply stated, *degradation* is the diminution of the biological productivity expected of a given tract of land. Degradation is keyed to human expectations, which vary by land use. Indeed, each type of land – farmland, wildland, or rangeland, for example – is nothing more than a set of expectations about the form its biota should take. The concept of degraded lands, therefore, is somewhat subjective, and a condition that constitutes degradation on a particular type of land may be considered normal elsewhere. (World Resources Institute and International Institute for Environment and Development, *World Resources 1988–89*, New York: Basic Books, 1989)

[An] environmental problem is defined as a degradation of natural capital and consequent decrease or loss of its service flows due to abuse/reduction of either the assimilative capacity or the regenerative capacity of the environment. Environmental problems vary in the degree of urgency depending on the trade-offs involved and the reversibility of action as new knowledge becomes available. Some natural capital losses may be more than compensated in terms of new man-made capital. However, other natural capital losses may be much larger than the corresponding gains in man-made capital. Critical environmental problems involve large losses of natural capital with accompanying losses in vital non-market service flows and in the value of complementary man-made capital. (G. Foy and H. Daly, *Allocation, Distribution and Scale as Determinants of Environmental Degradation: Case Studies of Haiti, El Salvador and Costa Rica*, Washington DC; World Bank Environment Department Working Paper No. 19, September 1989)

Desertification is a process of sustained land (soil and vegetation) degradation in arid, semi-arid and dry sub-humid areas, caused at least partly by man. It reduces productive potential to an extent which can neither be readily reversed by removing the cause nor easily reclaimed without substantial investment. (R. Nelson, *Dryland Management: The "Desertification" Problem*, Washington DC; World Bank Environment Department Working Paper No. 8, September 1988) or indirectly, currently or over time.

Perhaps the most difficult feature of environmental degradation is that its costs often occur *externally* to any market system and involve complex processes of ecological–economic interaction. Both the economic *causes* and the *effects* of environmental degradation are difficult to discern and analyse in developing countries.

Box 6.2 illustrates this problem by tracing out the diverse impacts of upper watershed degradation in Java, Indonesia. Long-term development problems such as population growth, rural unemployment, poverty and loss of traditional sustainable agricultural practices are at the root cause of a vicious circle of low income and low productivity in the uplands of Java. The result is increased cultivation on steep slopes, inappropriate cropping patterns and lack of investment in conservation measures – all of which are fundamental causes of soil fertility losses and erosion. Existing economic and agricultural policies in Indonesia – particularly subsidies for agricultural inputs and investment strategies for research, extension and infrastructure – are currently biased towards lowland irrigated rice production, and do little to assist the control of upper watershed degradation (Barbier, 1989, ch. 7).

The welfare impacts of upland degradation occur both *on-site* and *off-site*. The on-site impacts are usually manifested in terms of losses of agricultural output as land productivity, and thus crop yields, decline. In the Java uplands, low-value annual crops (maize, cassava) on steep slopes with sedimentary soils are particularly affected. As this characterizes much of the marginal land and cropping systems farmed by the poorest groups in the uplands, they are the most affected by soil erosion. The resulting income losses increase the poverty of these farmers, reinforce their need for short-term, unsustainable cultivation of the land, and ensure that insufficient capital is necessary for investments in soil conservation.

The off-site effects of upland soil erosion are more difficult to trace, but may nevertheless be extremely pervasive. These off-site impacts are literally "downstream". The soil runoff and increased sedimentation from the uplands lead to:

Box 6.2   Impacts of Upper Watershed Degradation – Java

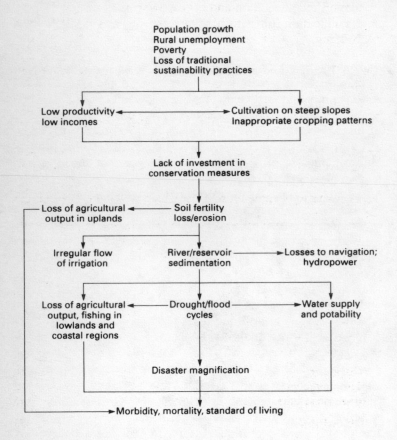

Source: E. Barbier, "The Contribution of Environmental and Resource Economics to an Economics of Sustainable Development", *Development and Change*, vol. 20, no. 3, July 1989, pp. 429–59.

- disruptions lower down the watershed to irrigation, dams and water systems and supply;
- losses to agriculture, aquaculture and fishing in the lowlands;
- disruptions to estuarine and coastal fisheries;
- diminished navigation and hydropower; and
- magnification of natural disasters, such as drought and flooding.

Box 6.3 shows one estimate of the costs of upper watershed degradation.

The impacts of environmental degradation are made even more complex by the *dynamic* nature of these economic–ecological interactions. Box 6.4 gives an example of the interactions between resource abuse enforced by poverty and the consequences of drought in the West African Sahelian and Sudanian zones. Over the long term, the rural production systems in the area appear to become more vulnerable to drought. Drought by

---

Box 6.3   **Costs of Watershed Degradation – Java**

The Costs of Soil Erosion on Java
(us$ million, 1987 prices)

On-Site Costs	315
Loss of agricultural output in uplands	
Off-Site Costs	58
Siltation of irrigation	10
Harbour dredging	2
Reservoir sedimentation	46
Total Soil Erosion	373
% Agricultural GDP	2.9
% GDP	0.4

Source: W. Magrath and P. Arens, *The Costs of Soil Erosion on Java: A Natural Resource Accounting Approach*, Environment Department, Working Paper No. 18, World Bank, Washington, DC 1989.

Box 6.4   **Drought and Environmental Degradation in the West African Sudano-Sahelian Zones**

The spread of rain-fed, extensive agriculture into forest, bush and pasture areas reduces total forage available to transhumant livestock, particularly when, as now, mixed farmers increasingly collect and stock crop residues to carry their own animals through the dry season period. When drought strikes, transhumant pastoralists do what they can to save herds. Lacking alternative forms of forage, they try to increase their animals' intake of browse. They vigorously lop trees already weakened by lack of soil moisture. Many trees die as a result of this abuse. Pressure then intensifies on the remaining woodstock during the next drought. Clearing fields for animal traction or machine cultivation may disrupt existing soil fertilization cycles based on nutrients that in-field trees return to the soil surface in the form of humus. If these organic nutrients are not replaced by organic and/or chemical fertilizers, crop yields decline. Stripping trees from fields also reduces the windbreak effect that even an open canopy can provide, and increases wind erosion. When fields are fallowed, in those systems where man/land ratios still permit it, natural regeneration occurs much more slowly. In the meantime, soils may suffer both wind and water erosion.

Source: World Bank, *Desertification in the Sahelian and Sudanian Zones of West Africa*, World Bank, Washington, DC, 1985.

---

itself does not pose a threat to the long-term sustainability of rural production systems, but it accelerates the negative consequences of environmental degradation resulting from poverty.

Local people are usually very much aware of the costs and impacts of environmental degradation. Indigenous knowledge of local farming systems, practices and agro-ecological conditions is, unfortunately, often overlooked in efforts to develop agriculture. Inappropriate, environmentally damaging agricultural systems and practices may result. Box 6.5 records the perceptions of older farmers in a district of southern Zimbabwe of how changes in land use have accounted for the present soil erosion problems

---

Box 6.5   **The Role of Trees in Eliminating Erosion – A Local View**

Mr Nhongo said that during the early colonial era, when shifting cultivation developed in sandy soil parts of this area [Mazvihwa, a semi-arid area of "red soils" in Zvishavane District, southern Zimbabwe], many trees were left in fields which maintained soil organic matter reducing erosion . . . . According to Nhongo, sandveld land was not farmed until it was exhausted and hence easily eroded, but fallowed after about five years to keep the soil strong. Trees were a necessary part of maintaining the soil. Excessive farming without trees, it was argued, led to topsoil loss, exposing an even more vulnerable sub-soil. This is why so much erosion was in old field areas. "It is the bareness and looseness of the worked out soil . . . which is causing this phenomenon of drainage development which we are so concerned about", said Mr Mambudzi. Extension workers have rigorously imposed tree removal from fields since the 1930s.

Source: K.B. Wilson, "Indigenous Conservation in Zimbabwe: Soil Erosion, Land-use Planning and Rural Life", paper submitted to the Panel Session "Conservation and Rural People", African Studies Association of UK Conference, Cambridge, 14 September, 1988.

The Economic Costs of Environmental Degradation

In Box 6.5 it is noted that the villagers appreciate the *total economic value* of trees, but government agricultural extension workers viewed trees as a hindrance to development of the land. The concept of total economic value (TEV) was introduced in *Blueprint 1* (see Pearce, Markandya and Barbier, 1989, ch. 3). This concept is just as valid to decisions affecting the environment in developing countries as in industrialized nations. As noted in *Blueprint 1*, the *full potential* TEV of any environmental resource or resource system should be:

$$\text{TEV} = \text{Actual Use Value} + \text{Option Value} + \text{Existence Value}$$

Actual use values are derived from use of the environment, whether direct or indirect. Direct use of the environment would be, for example, the use of trees for fodder or fuelwood. Indirect use would be the use of the nitrogen-fixing or soil-cohesion and water-retention properties of trees to boost crop yields and reduce soil erosion.

In addition to present use values of natural resources and ecological functions, individuals might also see the environment as providing potential benefits in the future. For example, in Box 6.5 the farmers appear to be expressing a preference to preserve the soil conservation and browsing functions of trees today as insurance against the risk of losing these functions, which might prove valuable in the future. Economists refer to this as *option value*, which will most probably be significant if individuals are averse to risk, if the future value of the environmental functions and resources are expected to be high even if currently unknown, and if environmental degradation is irreversible. In developing countries, option values may be of particular importance to indigenous peoples – forest-dwellers, traditional pastoral societies, artisanal fishing communities – whose whole culture and heritage is dependent on the unique attributes of the natural environment around them.

Existence values are values completely unrelated to use. For example, some people may derive satisfaction just from knowing that certain natural resource systems and environments exist and will be preserved. Existence values are closely bound up with the *uniqueness* of natural environments. We usually consider individuals outside developing countries – such as Westerners concerned over the fate of tropical forests – as holding existence values. Even within developing countries, however, an urban dweller may, for example, also consider certain natural environments, such as a unique tropical forest or wetland system, or even particular species (e.g. the "big five" – rhino, elephant, buffalo, lion and leopard – in Africa) as important for preserving even if he or she is never likely to see or use them.

As indicated in Box 6.5, the failure to appreciate and assess the total economic value of natural resources and functions is often the major factor behind environmental degradation. The result is often a *distortion* in *economic incentives*. That is, *the private costs of actions leading to environmental degradation do not reflect the full social costs of degradation, in terms of the environmental values forgone*. The full social costs of environmental degradation are what economists call *opportunity costs*. In the case of environmental degradation, the opportunity costs must be the losses to society of the use, option and existence values discussed above.

Excessive degradation of the environment and natural resources is *the outcome of their values not being fully recognized and integrated into decision-making processes by individuals in the marketplace and by governments*. If markets fail fully to reflect environmental values, *market failure* is said to exist. Where government decisions or policies do not fully reflect these values, there is policy or *government failure*. Throughout the developing world, the existence of poorly formulated input and output pricing policies, insecure land titling and registration, tax thresholds and rebates, cheap and restricted credit facilities, overvalued exchange rates and other policy distortions, has exacerbated problems of natural resource management. By failing to make markets and private decision-makers accountable for forgone environmental values, these policies may contribute to market failure. At worst, the direct private costs of resource-using activities are subsidized and/or distorted, thus encouraging unecessary environmental degradation.

Resource Rights as Incentives

Appropriate incentive structures must be set against the context of management regimes – access and rights to land and other resources – and the complexity of poverty–environmental degradation linkages in developing countries.

Throughout the developing world, broadly three types of resource management regimes exist – *private ownership*, *common property* and *open access*. In private ownership, resource rights and ownership are conferred on a private individual or group of individuals. For example, much farmland in developing countries is privately owned. Common property is the ownership and management of resources by a reasonably well-defined community. Often, communities will jointly own grazing land, forest, woodlots and even farmland. For example, in Malawi virtually all the agricultural land employed for food production is under customary ownership.

A frequent misperception is that common property leads to overexploitation by individuals – the "tragedy of the commons". However, many common property regimes involve the sustainable use of resources, but may break down owing to overpopulation or policy failures. This is frequently a problem for community-owned forests and grazing land, where controlling incursions is difficult. The result may be situations resembling "open access", where little common management or ownership exists. Open access does increase the risks of resource degradation, which highlights the requirement for some form of property rights or common management. Theoretically, privatization can conserve resources, but outcomes are less certain if private owners discount the future or if conditions of market and government failure persist.

Poverty, insecure and unsustainable livelihoods, uneven income distribution, and unequal access to assets, resources and inputs (including credit) are all contributory factors that accelerate environmental degradation. The dynamics between poverty and environmental degradation are not well understood. Regardless of the specific causes, once the cumulative causation process between poverty and environmental degradation sets in, risk and uncertainty become engrained in economic activities. As the environment deteriorates, poor rural households are constrained to shorter time horizons and restricted choices. The increased risk and uncertainty over livelihood security will tend to make poor households reluctant to change their farming practices, grazing patterns and other economic activities if, in the short run, these changes are perceived as adding to the risk burden. Poor farmers and pastoralists may be unwilling to bear the additional short-term risk of altering their choice of crops, input mixes, grazing patterns or other required practices, even if such changes improve their well-being over the long run. How-

Box 6.6   **Valuing the Benefits of Wetlands**

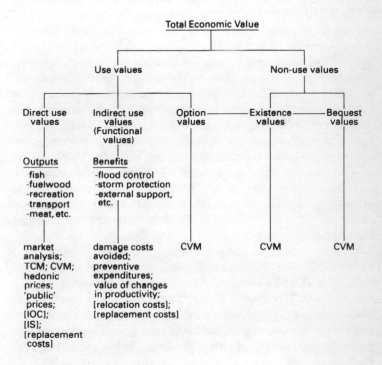

Notes: CVM = contingent valuation method
TCM = travel cost method
IOC = indirect opportunity cost approach
IS   = indirect sustitute approach
[ ] = valuation methodology to be used with care

Source: E. Barbier, *The Economic Value of Ecosystems: 1.–Tropical Wetlands*, LEEC Gatekeeper 89-02, London Environmental Economics Centre, London, 1989.

ever, the links between poverty and environmental degradation should not detract from other contributory factors: public and market failure, population pressures, migration and settlement patterns, infrastructure investments, and so on (Barbier, 1989; Conway and Barbier, 1990; Jagannathan, 1989).

Wetlands

The fate of the world's wetlands illustrates the previous arguments about value, resource rights and incentives. Since 1900, over half of the world's wetlands may have disappeared. The United States alone has lost an estimated 54 per cent (87 million hectares) of its original wetlands, of which 87 per cent has been lost to agricultural development, 8 per cent to urban development and 5 per cent to other conversions (Maltby, 1986, p. 90). The total area and status of tropical wetlands are still unknown, but the available evidence suggests that the pattern of wetland conversion in Third World countries may be similar to that of the United States – and perhaps proceeding at even a faster rate in some regions.

Natural wetlands perform many important functions for humankind – storm prevention, flood and water-flow control, nutrient and waste absorption, and so forth. Wetlands can also be used for recreation and water transport, and their diverse resources can be directly exploited for fishing, agriculture, wildlife products, wood products and water supply. When properly measured, the total economic value of a wetland''s ecological functions, services and resources may exceed the economic gains of converting the area to an alternative use. Some economic studies have valued the benefits of *temperate* wetlands (see Turner, 1988; Farber and Constanza, 1987).

But to date, little analysis of *tropical* wetland benefits has been undertaken. The methodology for economic valuation of tropical wetland resources is relatively straightforward, usually involving the value of the production gained by directly exploiting these resources (see Box 6.6). For example, in Hadeijia-Jama'are Floodplain, Nigeria, the total value of the annual production was Naira (N) 250–850 million for agriculture, N

Box 6.7 Comparative Benefits of Wetland and Irrigation, Tunisia

Lake Ichkeul and its associated marshes Djebel Ichkeul in Tunisia were gazetted as a national park in 1980. The main aim was to protect wildlife, particularly birds, but the park area also provides important direct grazing and fishing uses for local communities. However, despite its importance, Ichkeul is threatened by the construction of six dams on the rivers that flow into it. Two of these are already completed, a third is under construction and three others are scheduled for after the year 2000. The water is to be used for drinking and irrigation in the much drier south of Tunisia, and for irrigation in the floodplains of the Ghezala perimeter bordering the lake. Most of the water from the dams is currently being used for the latter purpose.

In order to determine the relative benefits of using water for agricultural irrigation compared to its use when released into the national park, the following analysis calculating the profit per cubic metre (m^3) of water was undertaken:

Comparative Returns of Wetland Uses to Irrigation
Ghezala and Ichkeul, Tunisia
(us$ 1987/8)

	Agricultural Irrigation, Ghezala	*Fisheries and Grazing Ichkeul National Park*		
Average annual water requirement (m^3)	0.53	1.8	4.4	12.0
Gross annual revenue per m^3 of water	0.293	0.358	0.146	0.054
Net annual costs per m^3 of water	0.356	0.031	0.012	0.005
Net annual profit per m^3 of water	−0.063	0.327	0.134	0.049

The table indicates that the gross annual income per m^3 of water released into the park is not as high as that obtained on agricultural land. However, because of the high relative costs of the agricultural

Box 6.7   **Continued**

system, the net annual profit of irrigation is negative, and always less than that of grazing and fishing in the park. The economic case for conserving the park is even stronger than this.

Fisheries and grazing are just two of the values of the national park. Other values include:

- *tourism* – in a five-week period in 1988, there were 2500 visitors to the park, of whom over 200 were from abroad;
- *desalinization of the water table* -- the wetlands assist in the water-table recharge from the rivers, whereas withdrawal of the water through the dams and irrigation schemes is likely to result in some salinization of the water table, which will severely reduce the quality of drinking water;
- *sewage treatment* – the marshes provide a free sewage treatment and water cleansing service for nearby towns;
- *control of birds* – loss of marshland has caused many birds to feed off farmland from the converted wetlands;
- *educational value* – in the five week period, 15 educational groups and one group comprising 312 students visited Ichkeul.

Source: D. Thomas, F. Ayache and T. Hollis, "Use Values and Non-Use Values in the Conservation of Ichkeul National Park, Tunisia", forthcoming in *Environmental Conservation*, 1990.

45 million for fishing and N 2 million for fuelwood (Kimmage and Adams, 1990). However, measuring the indirect benefits of wetland environmental functions, such as storm prevention and flood control, through damage-costs avoided and replacement costs is more problematic. More sophisticated techniques of contingent valuation, travel cost method and hedonic pricing are now increasingly being applied in developing regions – although not as yet to tropical wetlands valuation.

Box 6.7 illustrates how important it is to demonstrate the economic benefits of wetland areas if appropriate land-use decisions are to be made. In Ichkeul, Tunisia, the fishing and grazing benefits of the park alone are sufficient to justify preservation of the park when compared to diverting water from the wetlands to irrigation schemes along the perimeter. However, other values of the park – in terms of tourism, desalinization of the water table, sewage treatment, control of birds and educational value – may be even more significant.

The failure to account for the economic value of tropical wetland benefits, including the benefits derived by local communities dependent on natural wetlands, means that conversion in tropical wetlands will proceed in Third World countries as long as the economic gains from conversion – mainly for agricultural purposes – exceed the direct costs of drainage, clearing and other "reclamation" expenditures. As arable land becomes scarce in Third World countries, it is probable that subsidies and distortions to reduce the direct costs of wetland conversion may reach levels similar to those in OECD countries in the 1950s to 1970s. Efforts by the International Union for the Conservation of Nature, the Ramsar Convention Bureau and the International Waterfowl and Wetlands Research Bureau to co-operate on methodologies for wetland management, particularly in the hitherto neglected Third World, are welcomed. But the relevance of such efforts in affecting government development decisions and planning will depend crucially on improving and extending the economic evaluation of tropical wetlands.

Drylands

The term "drylands" is usually applied to all arid and semi-arid zones, and to areas in the tropical sub-humid zone subject to the same degradation processes that occur on arid lands. Accounting for about one-third of global land and supporting a population of 850 million, the world's drylands are rapidly being degraded through population growth, overgrazing, cropping on marginal lands, inappropriate irrigation and devegetation. The process of dryland degradation is often referred to as "desertification", where the productive potential of the land is reduced to such an extent that it can neither be readily reversed by removing the cause nor easily reclaimed without substantial investment.

There are few economic studies of the costs of dryland degradation. Those that exist – conducted mainly in OECD countries – suggest that the problem is signficant. For example, the annual cost of degradation in Canada's prairie region is estimated to

---

Box 6.8   Costs of Dryland Degradation, Burkina Faso

Although detailed assessment of the costs of dryland degradation in developing countries is difficult, some "best-guess" calculations are shedding light on the magnitude of the problem. In one study, for Burkina Faso, estimates were made of the total amount of biomass lost each year in the form of fuelwood and vegetation, which were translated into forgone household energy (fuelwood) valued at market prices, forgone millet and sorghum crops valued at market prices, and reduced livestock yield due to fodder losses:

Crop, Livestock and Fuelwood Losses, Burkina Faso

	Fuelwood loss (m³)	Livestock loss (UGB)[1]	Cereal loss (tonnes)
Sahel	0	175,000	19,000
Plateau Central	900,000	26,000	260,000
Sudano-Guinean	1,200,000	0	27,360
Total	2,100,000	201,000	306,360
Prices CFAF	22,258/m³	50,000/UGB	50,000/tonne
Values CFAF billion	46.7	10.0	15.3

Total Damage Costs = 72 billion CFAF = 8.8% of GDP

Notes: 1. UGB = Unites de Gros Bétail, a standardized livestock unit measure.

Source: D. W. Pearce and J. Warford, *Environment and Economic Development: The Sustainable Management of Natural Resources in the Developing World*, forthcoming, 1991, based on data from D. Lallement, *Burkina Faso: Economic Issues in Renewable Natural Resource Management*, Agricultural Operations, Sahelian Department, Africa Region, World Bank, Washington DC, 1990.

be US $622 million (Dixon, James and Sherman, 1989). Some work on the costs of dryland degradation in developing regions has been undertaken. Box 6.8 includes preliminary estimates of the costs of crop, livestock and fuelwood losses from dryland degradation in Burkina Faso.

Even less well developed is the analysis of the effects of economic and resource management *policies* on dryland degradation in Third World countries. This is often attributed to the superficial identification of the causes of desertification and to the frequently poor identification of the causes of the failures of dryland projects (Nelson, 1988). Although the majority of "causes" are attributable to population growth and natural events, dryland degradation is also symptomatic of an agricultural development bias that distorts agricultural pricing, investment flows, research and development, and infrastructure towards more "favoured" agricultural land and systems (Barbier, 1989). Where drylands "development" is encouraged, it is usually through the introduction of large-scale commercial agricultural schemes that can conflict with more traditional farming and pastoral systems.

The complexity of social, economic and environmental relationships is formidable. Not enough is often known about dryland farming and pastoral systems; open access use and common property resource rights; land tenure regimes and security; the distribution of wealth and income; and coping strategies under the presence of variable climatic conditions, frequent drought, market instability, political conflicts and other factors influencing risk and uncertainty. A common misperception is that the extension of private property rights, commercial agriculture and markets will "automatically" solve dryland management problems in the long run. At the same time, not all dryland farmers and pastoralists, even in the most distant and resource-poor regions, are totally isolated from agricultural markets. Virtually all subsistence households require some regular market income for cash purchases of some agricultural inputs and basic necessities; many farmers and pastoralists provide important cash and export crops. As a result, alterations in market conditions – whether from changes

Box 6.9   The Economics of Rehabilitating the Gum Belt, Sudan

In recent decades, the real producer price of gum arabic in Sudan has fluctuated considerably, as has the relative price of gum to its competitor cash crops (sesame, groundnuts) and even food crops (sorghum, millet). Farmers' share of the export value of gum also remains low: this has been one reason for the recent increase in smuggling of gum to neighbouring countries.

An economic analysis was conducted of six representative cropping systems containing gum arabic cultivation in Sudan. The results are indicated in the following table.

Economic Analysis of Six Cropping Systems, Sudan
(Sudanese Pounds per Feddan, 10% Discount Rate)

	Acacia Senegal[1]	Sorghum	Millet	Ground-nuts	Sesame	ALL CROPS
BN	2989.57	4606.83	2931.58			10527.98
WN	3923.82	−432.99	486.30	5330.92	8605.12	17913.17
NK	1471.36		2091.77		6020.94	9584.07
SK	882.99	1644.44		13109.44	13776.95	29413.82
ND	1240.87		2363.89	9687.69		13292.45
SD	1884.02	3830.80	3775.60	9715.61		19206.03
ALL	2065.44	2412.27	2392.83	9460.92	9467.67	16656.25

Notes: BN = Blue Nile Province, clay soils, largeholder
WN = White Nile Province, sandy soils, smallholder
NK = North Kordofan Province, sandy soils, smallholder
SK = South Kordofan Province, clay soils, largeholder
ND = North Darfur Province, sandy soils, smallholder
SD = South Darfur Province, sandy soils, smallholder
ALL = Average of all six systems

[1] Total NPV from gum, fuelwood and fodder, except for Blue Nile and South Kordofan (gum only).

Although the analysis shows that all six systems are economically profitable, the *relative profitability* of gum compared to other crops in each system is generally lower than that of other crops – except in the Tendelti system of the White Nile, where field crop damage occurs frequently. In most systems there are initial losses due to the need to establish gum gardens before they begin producing. This would suggest that *maintaining the real producer price of gum,* as was

Box 6.9 **Continued**

assumed in the analysis, is a necessary economic incentive to encourage gum cultivation.

However, despite the lower relative returns to cultivating gum arabic, there are several reasons why converting land under *A. senegal* to cultivating annual crops may not be desirable:

- some land under *A. senegal* may not be suitable for growing annual crops, resulting in very low and fluctuating yields;
- fallowing land may be important to maintain its fertility – gum arabic is the ideal cash crop for this purpose;
- the *environmental benefits* of gum arabic trees (e.g. control of erosion/runoff, windbreaks, dune fixation, nitrogen fixation) were not included in the analysis, and these maybe significant in maintaining the yields of field crops within the farming systems;
- risk-averse farmers may prefer that some of their land is held under gum cultivation, because the returns to gum – although lower than the maximum expected returns from the cash crops – may be less variable under stressful environmental and climatic conditions;
- gum cultivation provides cash income to farmers outside the growing season for cash crops.

Source: E. Barbier, *The Economics of Controlling Degradation: Rehabilitating Gum Arabic Systems in Sudan*, LEEC Paper 90-03, London Environmental Economics Centre, London, 1990.

in policies, climatic conditions, research and development innovations, or other factors – do have a significant impact on the livelihoods of rural groups in dryland areas. Understanding the responses to these changing market conditions is a crucial aspect of the dryland management problem.

The case of gum arabic production in Sudan illustrates these points. Gum arabic, which is produced from the *Acacia senegal* tree, is widely sought after in industrialized countries for use in confectionery and beverages, pharmaceuticals, artistic materials, photography, lithography, printing and pesticides. It is produced mainly in Sudan, and is that country's second largest export, earning over us \$65 million in 1987. In addition, *A. senegal* serves a variety of other valuable economic and ecological functions. These include fodder for livestock, fuelwood from older trees, reducing soil erosion and water runoff, nitrogen fixation, dune fixation and serving as windbreaks. Over wide stretches of the Northern Sudano-Sahelian zone, the presence of a gum arabic "belt" acts as a buffer against desertification.

However, fluctuations in the real price of gum and its price relative to those of other agricultural crops have had important impacts on farmers' cropping patterns, diversification strategies and decisions to replant gum – with important consequences for Sudan's gum belt (see Box 6.9). Even though it is economically profitable *and* environmentally beneficial to grow gum, only when these economic incentives are properly dealt with by the government will rehabilitation of Sudan's important gum belt take place.

Irrigation

From 1950 to the mid-1980s, cropland under irrigation increased by over 3 per cent annually – from 94 to over 270 million hectares. Around 18 per cent of the world's cultivated land is irrigated, producing 33 per cent of the total harvest. The equivalent of us \$250 billion has already been spent to expand irrigation capacity in the Third World, and it is expected that an additional us \$100 billion will be spent between 1985 and 2000. Two-thirds of the world's irrigated lands are in Asia, where 38 per cent of additional food production to the year 2000 is anticipated to come from existing irrigated areas and 36 per cent from newly irrigated areas (Repetto, 1986).

Virtually all irrigation developments in the Third World are through public investments, which are heavily subsidized. Distributional considerations, political concerns and common perceptions of water as a "free good" have generally led to charges well below costs of supply. Revenues collected from farmers in most Third World countries often cover only 10–20 per cent of the building and operating costs of irrigation systems, usually failing to cover just operation and maintenance (O

Box 6.10 **Rent-seeking Behaviour in Irrigation**

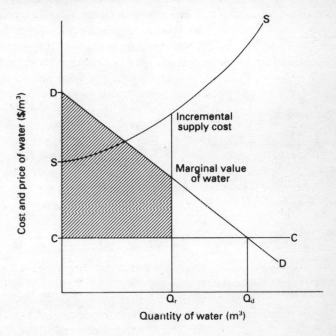

The failure to charge market-clearing prices for irrigation water gives rise to *rent-seeking*. Rent, or economic rent, is the difference between what the farmer would be willing to pay for irrigation water and what he actually pays. Because of price controls, these rents can frequently be very large. The diagram above illustrates the idea of economic rent. DD is a demand curve for irrigation water, SS a supply curve reflecting the costs of supply. Price is controlled at CC. Qr shows the rationed quantity of water – owing to the high demand at the subsidized prices, it is frequently necessary to ration the water between users. Rent at this level of supply is the difference between the demand curve, which shows the marginal value of water to the farmer, and the price charged – i.e. the shaded area in the diagram. Rents are in fact high in many Third World countries. The following table shows charges as a percentage of estimated farmer benefits in several countries.

Box 6.10 **Continued**

Economic Rents from Irrigation Schemes

Country	Estimated Benefits as % of $O + M + C$ costs	Economic Rents as % of Benefits
Indonesia		
high estimate of benefits	178	92
low estimate of benefits	65	79
Korea		
high estimate of benefits	71	74
low estimate of benefits	55	67
Mexico		
high estimate of benefits	NA	89
low estimate of benefits	NA	74
Nepal	135	95
Thailand	64	91
Philippines	233	90
Pakistan	NA	94

Note: $O + M + C$ costs are operational, maintenance and moderate capital costs.
Source: R. Repetto, *Skimming the Water: Rent-Seeking and the Performance of Public Irrigation Systems*, World Resources Institute, Washington, DC, 1986.

& M) costs alone. The result can be inefficient and poorly maintained irrigation networks, rent-seeking behaviour by farmers,
misallocation and wasteful use of water and unnecessary investments in major surface water developments, such as dams and
large-scale irrigation networks (see Box 6.10 on rent-seeking
behaviour in irrigation). The environmental impacts can be
significant:

(i) the disincentive to conserve water can lead to problems of
waterlogging, salinization and water scarcity; and
(ii) irrigation investments and infrastructure, including dams,
can lead to extensive external costs in the form of displacement
of local communities, loss of agricultural and forest lands; and

alterations in river hydrology, in fishing and wildlife industries and in erosion and sedimentation rates.

For example, in India 10 million hectares of irrigated land have been lost through waterlogging and 25 million are threatened by salinization; in Pakistan 12 million hectares are waterlogged and 5 million are saline (Repetto, 1986). Agricultural irrigation in Java accounts for about 47 per cent of the total potential water resources available and 75 per cent of the dry season/year flow. Given the expected future demands in all uses of water, the poor cost recovery and inefficiencies in irrigation (average efficiencies are 10–35 per cent and hardly exceed 30 per cent in most areas for both wet and dry seasons), water scarcity is becoming a chronic problem (World Bank, 1988). In Tunisia, an *ex post* analysis of the large-scale Ghezala irrigation project to take into account disruptive hydrological and other environmental impacts on the neighbouring Ichkeul National Park and surrounding areas reveals that these costs contribute to making the project economically unviable (See Box 6.7).

Land Degradation and Soil Erosion

Soil erosion and land degradation are not confined just to drylands and other marginal lands; the problem is pervasive throughout all agricultural systems, degraded forest lands, public and privately owned lands, and large- and smallholdings in the Third World. Moreover, soil erosion results from all forms of land degradation – overcropping, devegetation, deforestation, overgrazing, and so on. To simplify and limit the discussion, this section will discuss the problem of soil erosion and land degradation mainly in the context of *erosion of farm cropland*.

Reliable estimates of soil erosion are difficult. Little long-term monitoring of soil erosion from farmers' plots has occurred in Third World countries; aggregation and extrapolation from the few studies that do exist are fraught with complications. Regional – let alone national and international – comparisons should be treated with caution. Estimates of erosion based on the universal soil loss equation (USLE) and modified USLES adapted for tropical conditions still face many difficulties, as do methods involving Geographical Information Systems (GIS). To go further and analyse the impacts of erosion on crop yields or the impacts of runoff and sedimentation on "off-site" economic activities is even more difficult in Third World countries. Particularly frustrating is the fact that the declining trends in crop yields attributable to erosion are hard to substantiate, given that erosion impacts are often inseparable from the effects of climatic variations, relative price changes, changing cropping patterns, input mixes and labour use strategies, and so on.

Some recent studies of the economic costs of soil erosion indicate that these costs could be substantial. For example, in Mali current net farm income forgone from soil erosion is estimated to be US $4.6 to 18.7 million annually, and current plus future forgone income due to one year's soil erosion is estimated to be US $31 to 123 million (4–16 per cent of agricultural GDP). In Java, the on-site cost of soil erosion in upland areas is estimated to be around US $315 million annually (3 per cent of agricultural GDP), with additional off-site sedimentation costs of US $58 million (Bishop and Allen, 1989, and Box 6.2).

Another broad indicator of the costs of land degradation is the expenditure on recovery programmes to repair and reverse the effects. Box 6.11 details some of the upper watershed rehabilitation investments that the UN Food and Agriculture Organization expects to have spent between 1987 and 1991. The total expenditure over this period is expected to be around US $1 billion.

Designing appropriate policy responses to control soil erosion and land degradation is again hampered by the data limitations and the lack of microeconomic analyses of farmers' responses to erosion and incentives to adopt conservation measures. The limited evidence that does exist suggests that relationships – such as the effects of agricultural input and output pricing on farm-level erosion – are complex and difficult to substantiate. Nevertheless, there are some indications that subsidies for non-labour inputs, notably inorganic fertilizers, can artificially reduce the costs to farmers of soil erosion and,

Box 6.11 Rehabilitation Investments for Upper Watersheds and Semi-arid Lowlands in Selected Countries, 1987–91

Country	Recomended Programme	Investment Needed (million US dollars)
Colombia	Technical assistance, primarily training of management and extension staff, for watershed rehabilitation to protect hydropower investments	$50
Ethiopia	Technical assistance in preparation, training and organization of watershed rehabilitation projects in the Central Highlands Plateau region, soil conservation and provision of inputs to improve agricultural yields, and shelterbelts and on-farm tree planting on denuded areas	$100
India	Watershed rehabilitation treatment of 45 million hectares to protect the 18 out of 31 flood control reservoirs considered most urgently in danger of destruction by sedimentation, and tree-planting and rehabilitation of agricultural land at a cost of $250 per hectare	$500
Indonesia	Technical assistance in support of the government watershed management programme to improve agricultural productivity emphasizing tree crops, replant denuded areas of productive forest on steep slopes, and develop productive agricultural settlement on Sumatra, Kalimantan, and other islands. Expand watershed rehabilitation programme 50,000 hectares per year at $4 per hectare	$100
Kenya	Rehabilitation of 200,000 hectares of upland areas in the upper Tana River watershed through soil conservation, agricultural improvement, and tree-planting activities. Sediment control in semi-arid areas of the lower Tana River watershed through improved grazing and tree-planting	$35
Madagascar	Technical assistance for rehabilitation of degraded watersheds, including reforestation, soil conservation, and agricultural improvement, at $2 million per year	$10
Nepal	Technical assistance for panchayat forest development on 75 watersheds in the Middle Mountains, covering 375,000 hectares.	$15
Pakistan	Land-use reorganization, control, and rehabilitation of the lower watersheds above the Mangla and Tarbella dams, including reforestation of critical slopes with forage and fuelwood trees, terracing and improvement of permanent agriculture, and protection of forests	$45
Phillipines	Rehabilitation and protection of the 200,000 hectares of annually logged virgin forest to ensure regeneration of forest cover at $120 per hectare.	$120
Zimbabwe	Land-use reorganization and improvement in communal areas (grazing management, tree-planting, and irrigation schemes with watershed protection).	$46
Total		$1,021

Sources: Adapted from United Nations Food and Agriculture Organization (FAO). *Tropical Forestry Action Plan* (FAO, Rome, 1985). pp. 139–40. *Source*: World Resources Institute and International Institute for Environment and Development, *World Resources 1988–89*, Basic Books, New York, 1988.

on more resource-poor lands, substitute for manure, mulches and nitrogen-fixing crops that might be more appropriate. On the other hand, the *inaccessibility* of inorganic fertilizers – e.g. shortages caused by rationing cheap fertilizer imports – can lead to sub-optimal application and encourage farming practices that actually increase land degradation. Similarly, the relationship between erodibility and profitability of different cropping systems needs to be carefully analysed, particularly in relation to changing *relative prices* of different crops and changes in *real producer prices and incomes* over time. More complex incentive effects arise from the relationships between erosion and the availability of labour, off-farm employment, population pressure, tenure and access to frontier land, the development of post-harvesting capacity and other complementary infrastructure, and the availability of credit at affordable interest rates (Barbier, 1989, ch. 7; Conway and Barbier, 1990; Repetto, 1988; Pearce, Barbier and Markandya, 1990).

There are often strong economic incentives determining farmers' decisions to invest in soil conservation. Farmers will generally not modify their land-management practices and farming systems unless it is in their direct economic interest to do so. Such modifications are expensive and may involve risk. Unless soil erosion is perceived to be a threat to farm profitability – or alternatively, unless changes in land management lead to at least some immediate economic gains – farmers will be less willing to bear these substantial costs. In addition, the more productive or profitable the land use, the more farmers will be willing to maintain and invest in better land-management and erosion-control practices. Higher productivity and returns will also mean that farmers can afford to maintain terraces and other conservation structures and to continue with labour-intensive erosion-control measures. On the other hand, poorer farmers dependent on low-return cropping systems, such as maize or cassava, may be aware that soil erosion is reducing productivity but may not be able to afford to adopt conservation measures. At the other extreme, farmers with very profitable crops that are extremely erosive, such as temperate vegetables on steep upper volcanic slopes with deep topsoils, may not consider

Box 6.12 Women, Poverty and Land Degradation, Malawi

A. Smallholder Poverty Profile, Malawi

	Core Poor	Other Poor	Non–Poor
Sex of head of houshold (% female)	42	34	16
Number of labour days/ year – per household	532	606	762
Average landholding (ha) – per household	0.39	0.73	1.76
Agricultural services – % using fertilizer	9	16	35
– maize yield (1000 tn/ha)	1.2	1.3	1.4

B. Fertilizer Use by Household Type, Blantyre Agricultural Development Division, Malawi

Total Households		883		
Type of Household	*Male*		*Female*	
	No.	%	No.	%
	556	63.0	327	37.0
Fertilizer Farmers	208	37.4	90	27.5
Non-Fertilizer Farmers	348	62.6	237	72.5

C. Credit Disbursement and Input Use to Smallholders, Malawi

	83/84	84/85	85/86	86/87	87/88	88/89	89/90
Seasonal Loans ('000 Malawi Kwatcha)	11460	15555	19065	18283	26871	42211	57075
No. of Benefi- ciaries ('000)	180	212	208	206	243	301	315
Women as % of Beneficiaries	15.0	16.2	19.4	25.4	29.8	24.8	29.9

Box 6.12   **Continued**

D. *Adoption of Soil Conservation, Ntcheu Rural Development Project, Malawi*

Activity	Target	Achievement	(1/2)
	(1)	(2)	%
Farm Plans	M: 8	M: 3	37.5
	W: 2	W: 0	0.0
Contour Marker Ridges	M: 600	M: 232	38.7
	W: 300	W: 42	14.0
Composting	M:1500	M:1051	70.1
	W:1000	W: 156	15.6
Manuring	M:4500	M:3347	74.4
	W:2500	W:1002	40.1
Alley Cropping	M: 170	M: 30	17.6
	W: 80	W: 14	17.5
Buffer Strips	M: 8	M. 3	37.5
	W: 2	W: 0	0.0
Raised Boundaries/Paths	M: 200	M: 321	160.5
	W: 100	W: 199	199.0
Gully Reclamation	M: 80	M: 104	130.0
	W: 20	W: 20	100.0
Farmer Training	M: 500	M: 157	31.4
	W: 220	W: 245	111.4

Notes: M: Men, W: Women
Source: Table A from World Bank, *Malawi – Country Economic Memorandum: Growth Through Poverty Reduction,* Washington, DC, 1989, Table III.B.I; Tables B, C and D from E.B. Barbier and J.C Burgess, *Malawi – Land Degradation in Agriculture,* Report to the World Bank Economic Mission on Environmental Policy, Malawi, London July–August 1990.

soil conservation measures if their returns do not appear to be affected by soil erosion losses. Unfortunately, in most developing regions, we still do not have enough understanding of the economic and social factors determining these incentives for soil conservation.

Women and Land Management in Malawi[1]

In the agriculturally based economy of Malawi, declining soil fertility and soil erosion constitute a serious problem. The direct linkage between *women, poverty and the environment* is very strong (see Box 6.12). Female-headed households make up a large percentage (42 per cent) of the "core-poor" households. They typically cultivate very small plots of land (less than 0.5 hectares) and are often marginalized on to the less fertile soils and steeper slopes (more than 12 per cent). They are often unable to finance agricultural inputs such as fertilizer, to rotate annual crops, to use "green manure" crops or to undertake soil conservation. As a result, poorer female-headed households generally face declining soil fertility and lower crop yields, further exacerbating their poverty and increasing their dependence upon the land.

However, women's relationship with the environment is not just confined to the poverty link. Even in those households that are not classified as poor, the women are active participants in agricultural and household production. Thus, *women's use, perception, knowledge and management of the land* can be contrasted to that of men across all households. For example, a detailed study of the effects of agricultural commercialization among smallholders in the Zomba district of the southern region of Malawi emphasizes how the type of crops cultivated differ between men and women (Peters, Herrera and Randolph, 1989). Female-headed households on average cultivate the food crop maize on 90 per cent of their land and rarely grow any cash crops, whereas men grow maize on 81 per cent of their land, with the remainder mostly under the cash crop tobacco.

Women confront a multitude of *constraints* – non-existent or less binding for men – which hinder economic opportunities and improved land management. For example, both men and women may be constrained in uptaking new maize varieties, as they require relatively intensive fertilizer inputs as compared to traditional maize. However, female-headed households often have extremely low income and are unlikely to be able to raise sufficient financing from their own sources or to obtain credit to purchase hybrid maize and fertilizer (see Box 6.12). Large labour demands on women within the household – such as childbearing and rearing, fuel and water collection, cooking, land preparation, planting and weeding – further limit their ability to undertake sound land management – constructing ridging along contours, building bunds, maintaining buffer strips, planting trees, and so on. Off-farm employment opportunities for women to supplement farm income may also be constrained by gender discriminations in the labour market; for example, male labour is usually preferred to female labour for wage employment on tobacco estates.

Smallholders in Malawi appear to be aware of the problems posed by persistent soil erosion – especially farmers cultivating steep slopes, who frequently cite problems of runoff and declining yields. Extension advice on how to deal with the problems posed by soil erosion is generally reaching only larger, male farmers who are credit club members. Extension messages tend to be very general and are not customized to the needs and requirements of women, particularly the labour and other economic constraints they face. This is indicated in the relatively poor adoption of soil conservation measures by female as opposed to male farmers (see Box 6.12).

Conclusion

In *Blueprint 1* we argued that tackling environmental problems requires efforts to:

- modify the system of national accounts (SNA) to indicate how changes in the environment are linked to changes in the economy;
- correct market prices to reflect the full costs (and benefits) of "using" the environment;
- account more fully for the economic value of environmental impacts in the appraisal of projects.

Similar actions are required by developing countries to halt excessive environmental degradation. The existing data and information constraints would make wholescale modifications of the SNA for developing countries to account for all forms of environmental degradation impractical at this stage. Instead, a set of separate "satellite" environmental accounts should be established. For most developing countries, the first step is to compile consistent environmental and resource databases that could be used to indicate the linkages between the environment and economic activity. Eventually, these accounts could be extended to estimate a natural resource balance sheet leading to a measure of sustainable income. One approach, which has been applied to Indonesia for forests, petroleum and soils, is to account for the depreciation in the resource base (Repetto *et al.*, 1989). Almost half the average annual growth rate of 7.1 per cent between 1971 and 1984 in Indonesia was found to be "unsustainable" – i.e., involving depreciation of these critical resource stocks.

The "proper" pricing of environmental resources and functions should cover the full marginal social costs of their use. Correction of government and market failures in developing countries must be a priority where these failures give rise to excessive environmental degradation. The ultimate objective must be to develop appropriate incentives for private decision-makers. Improvements in *pricing*, or variable incentives, alone – altering input and output pricing, modifying the exchange rate, adjusting middlemen margins, and so on – may not be enough. Incentives focused on individual resource *users* (such as changes in land and resource rights, increased participation in decision-making and improved access to credit) or on the *policy-maker* (such as increasing institutional strength and co-ordination, improving the political climate and reducing corruption) may also prove necessary. The challenge for policy is to design the right combination of incentives for a given target group of individuals and environments.

Proper valuation of environmental resources and functions is also essential to analysis of specific project and programme investments in developing countries. A common misconception that must be avoided is that a direct economic use of a resource system (e.g. a mangrove wetland system), such as fuelwood, timber or fish harvesting, is more valuable than the system's ecological functions, such as storm protection or nutrient cycling. As the value of an ecological function is derived from its indirect support or protection of economic activity and property, it may be difficult to measure. The function may nevertheless prove extremely valuable over the long run. Individuals' preferences for preserving unique natural systems are often more problematic to evaluate, yet these preferences may be very strong.

Placing values on all these functions and resources may be constrained by insufficient data. In addition, a project-by-project appraisal approach may not be able to capture the "wider" environmental benefits, as the contribution of each project to the overall benefit might be marginal. For example, a single tree-planting project in semi-arid areas may be able to assist dune fixation, but many such stands are required to stop widespread desertification. Secondly, even if environmental benefits can be estimated, their impacts are often more significant in the long rather than the short term. The positive discount factor of a conventional economic analysis may therefore reduce the importance of these impacts in the project appraisal (Barbier, Markandya and Pearce, 1990; Markandya and Pearce, 1988).

In *Blueprint 1* we suggested the idea of an *environmentally compensating project*. That is, at least one project should be included that "compensates" for the environmental degradation generated by other projects in a portfolio of investments. In developing countries, many so-called environmental "rehabilitation" or "enhancement" projects, such as shelter-belt planting, soil conservation, afforestation and reforestation to control desertification, could serve as environmentally compensating projects. These projects would no longer need to be accepted on the basis of their discounted economic returns but on whether their stream of environmental benefits compensates for any environmental damages imposed by other projects.

Notes

1. This section was written with the assistance of Joanne C. Burgess, and is based on Barbier and Burgess (1990).

References

Barbier, E.B. (1989), *Economics, Natural-Resource Scarcity and Development: Conventional and Alternative Views*, London: Earthscan.

Barbier, E.B. and J.C. Burgess (1990), *Malawi – Land Degradation in Agriculture*, Report to the World Bank Economic Mission on the Environmental Policy, Malawi, London.

Barbier, E.B., A. Markandya, and D.W. Pearce (1990), "Sustainable Agricultural Development and Project Appraisal", *European Review of Agricultural Economics*, vol. 17, pp. 181–96.

Bishop, J. and J. Allen (1989), *The On-Site Costs of Soil Erosion in Mali*, Environment Department Working Paper No. 21, Washington, DC: World Bank.

Conway, G.R. and E.B. Barbier (1990), *After the Green Revolution: Sustainable Agriculture for Development*, London: Earthscan.

Dasgupta, P. (1982), *The Control of Resources*, Oxford: Basil Blackwell.

Dixon, J., D. James, and P. Sherman (1989), *The Economics of Dryland Management*, London: Earthscan.

Farber, S. and R. Constanza (1987), "The Economic Value of Wetland Systems", *Journal of Environmental Management*, vol. 24, pp. 41–51.

Jagannathan, N.V. (1989), *Poverty, Public Policies and the Environment*, Environment Department Working Paper No. 24, Washington, DC: World Bank.

Kimmage, K. and W.M. Adams (1990), *The Economic Value of Production in the Hadejia-Jama'are Floodplain, Nigeria*, A Report to the Co-ordinator, Wetlands Programme, IUCN, Cambridge: Department of Geography, University of Cambridge.

Markandya, A. and D.W. Pearce (1988), *Environmental Considerations and the Choice of the Discount Rate in Developing Countries*, Environment Department Working Paper No. 1, Washington, DC: World Bank

Nelson, R. (1988), *Dryland Management: The "Desertification" Problem*, Environment Department Working Paper No. 8, Washington, DC: World Bank.

Pearce, D.W., A. Markandya, and E.B. Barbier, (1989), *Blueprint for a Green Economy*, London: Earthscan.

Pearce, D.W., E.B. Barbier, and A. Markandya (1990), *Sustainable Development: Economics and Environment in the Third World*, London: Edward Elgar.

Peters, P.E., M.G. Herrera, and T.F. Randolph (1989), *Cash Cropping, Food Security and Nutrition: The Effects of Agricultural Commercialization Among Smallholders in Malawi*, Report to the US Agency for International Development, Harvard Institute for International Development, Cambridge, Massachusetts.

Repetto, R. (1986), *Skimming the Water: Rent-Seeking and the Performance of Public Irrigation Systems*, Washington, DC: World Resources Institute.

Repetto, R. (1988), *Economic Policy Reform for Natural Resource Conservation*, Environment Department Working Paper No. 4, Washington, DC: World Bank.

Repetto, R., W. Magrath, M. Wells, C. Beer, and F. Rossini (1989), *Wasting Assets: Natural Resources in National Income Accounts*, Washington, DC: World Resources Institute.

Turner, R.K. (1988), "Wetland Conservation: Economics and Ethics", Chapter 9 in D. Collard, D.W. Pearce and D. Ulph (eds), *Economics, Growth and Sustainable Development: Essays in Memory of Richard Lecomber*, London: Macmillan, pp. 121–59.

World Bank (1988), *Indonesia – Java: Water Resources Management Report*, Washington, DC: World Bank.

World Commission on Environment and Development (1987), *Our Common Future* ("The Brundtland Report"), Oxford University Press.

7

Population Growth

David Pearce

Introduction

One of the remarks made about *Blueprint for a Green Economy* was that we had failed to address the problem of world population growth. As Chapter 1 points out, *Blueprint 1* was not aimed at global environmental problems, but rather at the problems of a single country, the United Kingdom. While a good many people probably feel that the United Kingdom is overpopulated, "population control" is hardly a dominant issue in an economy in which population is tending towards a stable size. Globally, however, population growth is a major challenge, if not the major challenge, to sustainable development. The critics who suggested that we address the world population issue seemed occasionally to suggest that if we had no "solution" to world population growth, then the rest of what we had to say must be irrelevant. Unfortunately, those same people seemed to have no "solutions" either – or none that would be tolerated in a society in which there is some reverence for life. The "economic" approach offers few additional insights into practical policy means for lowering population growth. It is a matter of education, of persuasion, of making contraception widely and cheaply available, and of persuading those who find some moral obstacle to control that the social costs of their morality fall on many, many others who do not share that morality. Worse, the costs are borne most heavily by those who are least able to bear them. This chapter looks at the world population problem. Anyone seeking for a "new" solution to it may not wish to read any further. There are no new solutions.

World Population Growth

World population currently stands at some 5 billion people. By 2000 there will be 6 billion people and by 2025 over 8 billion. The *rate* of increase will peak in the early 1990s at about 88 million per annum. Total population growth and its regional distribution are shown in Box 7.1. Asia (excluding Japan) has the largest share of the world's population (56 per cent of the total), much of it in China (1040 million people) and India (765 million). The fastest rate of increase is in Africa.

A long-run historical perspective reveals that world population growth rates changed dramatically around the time of the Industrial Revolution in the developed world. In Europe the rate of change went from 0.5 per cent to 1.5 per cent per annum. In North America the rate rose to 2 per cent per annum in the early nineteenth century, owing to high fertility, low mortality and substantial immigration. Yet these are low

---

Box 7.1   **World Population Trends 1900–2100**

			(millions)			
	1900	*1950*	*1985*	*2000*	*2025*	*2100*
Africa	133	224	555	872	1617	2591
Asia[1]	867	1292	2697	3419	4403	4919
Latin America	70	165	405	546	779	1238
Total: Developing World	1070	1681	3657	4837	6799	8748
Europe, USSR, Japan, Oceania	478	669	917	987	1062	1055
North America	82	166	264	297	345	382
Total: Developed World	560	835	1181	1284	1407	1437
Total: World	1630	2516	4837	6122	8206	10,185

Notes: 1. Excludes Japan.
Source: T. W. Merrick, "World Population in Transition", *Population Bulletin*, vol. 42, no. 2, 1986.

rates of increase compared to the experience of developing countries in the twentieth century. Rates of growth below 2 per cent per annum have been the exception, with annual rates being closer to 3 per cent, twice that of the developed countries at a comparable stage of development. The marked contrast in historical experience is underlined by the fact that population growth and increases in material prosperity were correlated in the developed world transition, but population growth tends to be fastest the *poorer* the country in the current developing world. In short, there seems to be little by way of comparison between the historical experience of the currently developed countries and the recent experience of the developing world.

World population growth has resulted from marked reductions in mortality rates due to improved health care, education and sanitation, especially in the developing world. For example, a quarter of Sri Lanka's decline in mortality after 1945 has been attributed to malaria control.[1] While birth rates have also fallen, they remain significantly above death rates in the developing world and only slightly above in the developed world. It is this factor which provides the proximate explanation for the difference between developed and developing world experience. In the developed world, reductions in mortality rates were generally accompanied by reductions in birth rates. Reductions in birth rates in the developing world have lagged behind reduced mortality rates, and in a number of cases the birth rate has hardly fallen at all.

Why, then, should there be a historical difference between developed and developing world in the time profile of birth rates? The reasons are complex, and there appears to be no universally valid explanation for all countries. In Korea, fertility rates[2] fell by 44 per cent between 1965 and 1982 as women married later and later. The 1982 level has continued to fall, but at a much slower rate because the average age of women at marriage is tending towards a limit. The potential for further fertility decline is thus constrained. In Costa Rica, fertility rates fell by 48 per cent between 1965 and 1987, and are expected to fall by a further 25 per cent by 2000. But there are signs that there is some lower limit to the desired family size.

This suggests that fertility rates will not decline continuously, as they did in the developed world. The experience with family planning varies markedly. In India, the total fertility rate has fallen continuously, but contraceptive practice varies according to female literacy and the vigour with which policy is pursued.

Some insight into the reasons for the slower-than-expected decline in fertility in the developing world can be obtained by looking at the underlying factors involved in the African experience.

There is a special problem of population growth in Sub-Saharan Africa.[3] Whereas population growth rates are broadly constant or declining in all other regions of the world, growth rates in Sub-Saharan Africa (SSA) have increased steadily from 2.5 per cent per annum in 1960 to 3 per cent per annum in 1983. This is the outcome of significant reductions in death rates and very little change in birth rates (indeed, some countries have experienced increased birth rates). Ivory Coast, Zimbabwe and Kenya have growth rates in excess of 4 per cent per annum which, if sustained, would double their populations in less than eighteen years.[4] For Sub-Saharan Africa as a whole, the 1985 population of 485 million would be doubled in just twenty-two years if current rates of growth were sustained.

Mortality rates have fallen dramatically in SSA from just under 30 per 1000 in 1950 to some 16 per 1000 in the early 1980s. This decline reflects the general increase in living standards, education and public health programmes. The reasons for the constancy in the birth rate are found in underlying cultural attitudes to the bearing of children, and in economic factors. As health improves, so does natural fecundity (the physiological ability to bear children). Age at marriage for girls in Africa has not declined significantly. There is some evidence that breastfeeding and post-natal sexual abstinence have declined, and there is an extremely low use rate for contraceptives. The factors underlying these proximate reasons for the continued high birth rate appear to be as follows:[5]

(i) the continuing agricultural bias in African economies. This provides incentives to "invest" in children as labour on the farm: assisting with fuelwood and water collection, caring for children, looking after livestock, etc. Moreover, the amount of land that can be cultivated often depends on family size, creating further incentives for large families. The private benefits from increasing family size thus tend to outweigh the private costs, and this determines family size decisions. The net private benefits will tend to diminish, and eventually become negative above a limited family size, as education opportunities expand, as off-farm employment opportunities increase, and as land tenure and ownership patterns change. State-provided education incurs private costs in the form of uniforms, books and travel, making larger families more costly. Urban work opportunities reduce the need for on-farm labour, and tenurial change reduces the incentive to claim resource and land rights on the basis of family size;

(ii) larger families act as a form of social security through the extended family. Being a child frequently involves many obligations to other members of the family. Once again, "investing in children" becomes a way of ensuring care in old age. More generally, larger families mean wealth and influence. As state-provided social security systems are introduced, so this motive for larger families will weaken;

(iii) as long as women have an inferior social role to men, any preferences they might have for smaller families will be under-represented in the private cost-benefit decision about family size. Often, however, a woman's own status depends on childbearing, so that women appear to share the preference for large families. As education expands and other forms of emancipation increase, so some women might be expected to change their preferences for large families, while others, with a prevailing but overruled preference for smaller families, might be expected to exert more influence;

(iv) many cultures simply favour large families. Women are afforded more respect if they have more children, while barrenness may be regarded as a legitimate reason for divorce;

(v) having few children and investing in their education is a high-risk strategy if infant mortality is high and employment prospects are poor. Once again, this "risk aversion" influences the private cost-benefit decision in favour of large families. As employment prospects improve and infant mortality declines, the benefit:cost ratio can be expected to change to favour smaller families.

Clearly, the social, economic and cultural factors underlying decisions about family size are complex. They are also likely to vary from society to society. In general, however, the private benefit:cost ratio favours large families at low levels of education, high levels of rural dependence and low levels of state-provided social security. As these change, the ratio falls and favours smaller families. The obvious problem in SSA is that these factors are changing all too slowly relative to the factors reducing the death rate.

The Carrying Capacity of the Earth

Continued world population growth is inevitable. The means of controlling it require extensive efforts to influence birth rates, with all the consequent problems of addressing the underlying reasons for large family size. One reason for increasing that effort is to break the vicious circle of population growth and poverty. The influence of population growth on resource availability and environmental quality contributes to the poverty process. At the global level, more people mean a higher consumption of energy, and hence more atmospheric pollution, unless means are found by which to lower *per capita* consumption of materials and energy without impairing standards of living. More people mean a greater demand for cultivable and residential land, and hence less forest and wetlands, contributing to further pollution and losses of biodiversity.

One way of assessing the ultimate limits of population growth is to look at the *carrying capacity* of natural resources and land. Simply put, the carrying capacity of a given area is the maximum number of people that can be sustained by the resources on that land. The carrying capacity of a region is categorically not the *desirable* level of population, unless the level of well-being at which the population is sustained is itself desirable. Usually, however, carrying capacity is defined as relating to the maximum sustainable population at the minimum standard of living necessary for survival. For example, it is possible to compute the maximum food output (measured in calories, say) of a given area of land. Suppose this is represented by Q. Then Q can be divided by the minimum number of calories required for human survival of one individual. Call this M. Carrying capacity is then measured as:

$$Carrying\ Capacity = Q/M$$

The most extensive analysis of the carrying capacity of the world was carried out by the Food and Agriculture Organization (FAO) of the United Nations.[6] The FAO approach involved looking at the potential food production of each of 117 countries. Obviously, potential food production depends on the level of technology applied to agriculture. FAO categorized these as:

low-level: corresponding to no fertilizers, pesticides or herbicides, with traditional crop varieties and no long-term conservation measures;
intermediate-level: corresponding to use of basic fertilizers and biocides, use of some improved crop varieties and some basic conservation measures;
high-level: corresponding to full use of fertilizers and biocides, use of improved crop varieties, conservation measures and the best crop mixes.

On the basis of these different technological scenarios it was then possible to estimate the potential calorie output for each level of technology (Q in the equation). By dividing this by the *per capita* calorie intakes recommended by FAO and the World Health Organization for each country (M in the equation), a sustainable population can be estimated. These estimates were made for 1975 and the year 2000.

Box 7.2   **Carrying Capacities for World Regions in 2000**

(Potentially supportable population divided by expected population)

Input level	Africa	SW Asia	S America	C America	SE Asia	Average
Low	1.6	0.7	3.5	1.4	1.3	1.6
Intermediate	5.8	0.9	13.3	2.6	2.3	4.2
High	16.5	1.2	31.5	6.0	3.3	9.3

Source: FAO, *Land Food and People*, Rome, 1986, p. 16.

Box 7.2 shows the results in a convenient form. It shows the ratio of potential sustainable population in 2000 to the expected population in 2000 for various regions of the world, and at the three different levels of technology. For example, for the developing world as a whole, if all cultivable land was devoted to food crops, at the lowest level of technology those lands could support 1.6 times the number of people expected in the year 2000. In South-West Asia the actual expected population will exceed the carrying capacity at both low and intermediate technology levels. As the technological assumptions improve, so, dramatically, does the carrying capacity of the regions.

Box 7.2 appears to suggest a fairly optimistic picture. Certainly, it highlights the role which technological improvement can play in vastly increasing carrying capacity. However, it is important to understand why the picture is far from an optimistic one. There are several problems:

carrying capacity relates to the maximum number of people that can be sustained with the given resource, not to the desirable level;

the carrying capacity figures relate to a minimum calorie intake, so that even for a single person the approach makes no allowance for increasing nutritional levels;

the time horizon of 2000 does not permit much change to take place in levels of applied technology, so that at least the high-technology input scenario is of limited relevance to what will actually be the case;

the approach assumes that *all* cultivable land will come under food production or livestock pasture, which is a clear exaggeration of what is feasible. Allowing for non-food crops, the ratio of 1.6 in Box 7.2 becomes 1.07 – i.e. at low technology the carrying capacity of the developing countries is only 7 per cent more than the actual population.

In fact the situation may be worse even than this. The FAO study was concerned with carrying capacity in terms of *food*, but other resource scarcities may begin to exert an influence before cultivable land does. A notable example is the availability of fuelwood. A study of the Sahelian and Sudanian zones of

---

Box 7.3 Carrying Capacities in Sahelian/Sudanian Zones of West Africa

$(people/km^2)$

| Zone | Sustainable Population: | | | Actual Rural | Sustainable Population: | Actual Total |
	Crops	Live-stock	Sum		Fuelwood	
Saharan		0.3	0.3	0.3	–	0.3
Sahelo–Saharan		0.3	0.3	2	–	2
Sahelian	5	2	7	7	1	7
Sahelo–Sudanian	10	5	15	20	10	23
Sudanian	15	7	22	17	20	21
Sudano–Guinean	25	10	35	9	20	10

Source: D. Steeds, *Desertification in the Sahelian and Sudanian Zones of West Africa*, World Bank, Washington, DC, 1985, p. 13.

West Africa computed the carrying capacity of various zones according to the limits set by crops, livestock and fuelwood.[7] The results are shown in Box 7.3. It will be observed that the carrying capacity of natural forest cover – the main source of fuelwood – is very much lower than that of crops using traditional technologies. Moreover, in five of the six regions (underlined) fuelwood carrying capacity is already exceeded, compared to two regions where food and livestock carrying capacity is exceeded. The general picture on world zone carrying capacities may therefore understate the problem of resource carrying capacity generally. What matters is which resource scarcity "bites" first.

Carrying capacity calculations are helpful up to a point. They can be used to indicate the broad-scale seriousness of a problem, but there are considerable dangers in deriving too many conclusions from them. The main drawbacks are as follows:

at the country or small-region level, carrying capacity can be readily increased by trade. If we calculated the carrying capacity of, say, South Korea, it would show up adversely. Yet by trading on the basis of its comparative advantage in technology and industry, Korea can import food and so sustain a larger population;

as population grows, so there is a "forcing" effect on technology. It may, for example, lead to changes in the way in which agriculture is practised. Population growth generally explains the transition from shifting cultivation with long fallow periods, to short fallow farming and cropping rotations with organic manuring, to modern intensive monocultures based on high-yield crops, irrigation, fertilizers and chemicals. Carrying capacity tends to be a "static" concept, and thus cannot capture these dynamic, interactive effects.

Despite these drawbacks, a casual glance at the level of population – resource imbalance and the rate of agricultural growth suggests that the greater the pressure on natural resources, the slower agricultural growth becomes. This relationship for four groups of countries in Sub-Saharan Africa is shown on the next page:

Country Group	Agricultural Growth (% p.a.)
1	1.1
2	2.2
3	3.5
4	1.5

Group 1 relates to countries where actual population exceeded the sustainable population in 1982; Group 2 relates to countries where this will occur in 2000; group 3 to countries where it will happen in 2030; and group 4 to the remaining countries – i.e. those whose carrying capacities will not be exceeded by 2030. In all cases the measure of carrying capacity is that of the FAO. The data suggest that the closer a country is to its carrying capacity, the slower is its agricultural growth rate. In turn this suggests that the relationship between population growth and food output might reduce to the balance between two forces working in opposite directions: the role of population pressure in inducing technological inducement to higher productivity, and its role in wider resource degradation that reduces agricultural growth. The next section looks at these linkages.

Population Growth as a Cause of Technological Change

There are positive aspects to population growth. The evolution of agricultural systems is closely linked to changes in population density.[8] Given the extensive forest cover of land in the earliest stages of man's development, primitive hunter-gatherer societies gave way to forest fallow systems based on forest clearance, use of the cleared land for a few years, and then relocating elsewhere in new forest land. As population grew, so fallow periods shortened and forest cover declined in density, giving way to bush and shrub cover and then to grassland cover. Further population growth led to the abandonment of the fallow period altogether, necessitating the search for methods of restoring soil fertility which the fallow period had previously achieved naturally. For soil fertility to be sustained or improved, therefore, the soil's natural regenerative capacity obtained from the fallow period has to be substituted for by other inputs and by technology. One immediate reaction to declining fertility was – and is – increased labour inputs. Similar substitutions occur with organic manuring and, subsequently, artificial fertilizers, the use of animal draught power and, later still, mechanical power.

While this process describes the general transition from "extensive" to "intensive" agriculture, it is important to recognize that some agro-ecosystems cannot support intensive farming technologies. Some soils are quickly eroded by mechanical tillage, for example. Thus the picture of agricultural development as a competing process between soil degradation brought on by the loss of natural regeneration (due to declining fallow periods) and technological advance has to be tempered by consideration of the types of soil and ecosystem in place. To put it another way: intensification and labour productivity are not necessarily closely correlated. Moreover, empirical tests of the various linkages involved are not conclusive, although there does appear to be a close correlation between population density and farming intensity. The other linkage is between declining fallows and agricultural productivity. Various studies establish this relationship, although data for Sub-Saharan Africa, where the advance of technology to compensate for declining fertility has been conspicuously slow, tend to be sparse.[9]

The process therefore seems to be that population growth leads to reduced fallow periods and increased farming intensity. This, in turn, reduces soil productivity. Farmers react by introducing technological change. The relative speed at which technology changes compared to the decline in soil productivity and the increase in population growth determines the rate of change in agricultural productivity. In terms of carrying capacity arguments, technological change shifts the carrying capacity by enabling the land to support ever larger population levels. Population growth may thus "force" technological change and increase agricultural productivity, and hence food supplies. It may also cause declining productivity if, for any number of reasons, technological change does not take place. One reason why technological change may not occur is if the soils in question cannot support such changes. If there are such "limits to technology" it then matters a great deal that the final farming system established has the capability of trading with other areas. For example, areas with soils suited only to rangelands may trade livestock with areas suited to arable crops and more intensive farming.

What are the policy implications of these probable linkages between population growth, technology and soil fertility ? It is tempting to draw a *"laissez faire"* conclusion: there is no need to intervene to reduce population growth rates because they will generate feedback effects which will ultimately increase food production. This is a dangerous conclusion. As we have seen, there is nothing in the argument to prove that rates of technological change will be *sufficient* to outweigh the deleterious effects of population growth on soil productivity. To observe that they have had this effect in the past carries no particular implication for what will happen in the future, not least because the "agricultural revolution" required has to take place in different climatic conditions. Second, even where technology does achieve marked increases, as with the "green revolution", the technology itself can have significant negative environmental consequences – the effects of fertilizer runoff on water systems, pesticides on human health, and monocultural cropping on the resilience of ecosystems to shock and stress. Third, and perhaps most significant, if the technological change can be secured *without* rapid population growth, this is surely better than technological change *with* population growth. The fallacy in the optimistic interpretation of the population–agriculture linkage is in seeing population growth as a *necessary condition* for improved agricultural productivity.

For these reasons at least, policy has to continue to be directed towards *both* improving the application of technology *and* reducing population growth rates.

Resources and Population Growth

(a) Net Primary Product
Implicit in the previous analysis was a linkage between population growth and use of the total land area available for different

uses. As population grows and fallow periods decline, so any existing plot of land is "occupied" on an increasingly continuous basis. If efforts are made to colonize hitherto uncultivated land, so the land available for other uses declines. The "other uses" here include recreational use, wildlife habitat and general environmental protective functions. One consequence of population growth, then, is that resources other than agricultural land fertility disappear. Ecologists characterize this effect in terms of competing uses for "Net Primary Production" (NPP) in the world's ecosystems. NPP is the change in the world's biomass due to the fixing of solar energy by the photosynthetic conversion of CO_2 into usable carbon compounds. Approximate calculations suggest that the standing stock of biomass in the world is about 1800×10^{15} grams, and that NPP is around 175×10^{15} grams per annum.[10] Estimates put the amount of *terrestrial* NPP used for food, fuel, timber and fibre for people, together with losses of NPP due to human alteration of ecosystems, at about 40 per cent, and the appropriation of terrestrial and aquatic NPP at 25 per cent.[11] The significance of this ecological view is that population growth is increasing this proportion by (a) increasing the amount of NPP needed to support food production, and (b) reducing NPP through forest clearance and conversion to agriculture. Note that (b) occurs because agricultural land contributes less NPP than forested land – i.e. a reduction in forest is not compensated wholly by its conversion to agriculture.

Some authors have noted the potentially alarming consequences of these levels of NPP appropriation. Taking the 25 per cent figure, for example, means that two more "doubling times" of the human population would, at the same resource-*per-capita* rate, mean 100 per cent appropriation of NPP, an ecological impossibility. Yet one doubling time is expected to occur before the end of the twenty-first century.[12]

(b) Non-Renewable Resources

As population expands, so we can expect the demand for non-renewable resources, such as coal, oil and metal ores, to rise. But consumption *per capita* is also likely to rise as living

Box 7.4 **Population Growth and Energy Consumption, 1960–84**

Region	% of Increased Energy Consumption due to:			Energy Consumption per capita:[1]	
	Population	Living Standards		1960	1984
World	46	54		38	55
Africa	33	67		6	12
N America	51	49	USA	236	281
			Canada	164	286
S America	37	63		16	28
Asia	18	82		8	20
Europe	16	84		72	124

Notes: 1. 10^9 joules per person.
Source: computed from data in United Nations Environment Programme, *Environmental Data Report*, Blackwell, Oxford, 1987.

standards improve. Box 7.4 illustrates the relative contributions of population growth and rising *per capita* consumption levels on the demand for commercial energy (i.e. energy excluding woodfuels and other biomass energy). The relative contributions are computed by taking the *per capita* energy consumption level for 1960 and multiplying it by the 1984 population level. This shows what the energy consumption level *would have been* had *per capita* consumption remained unchanged with population growth. This change in the total energy consumed is then expressed as a percentage of the total *actual* change in energy consumption between 1960 and 1984.[13] The data also show the *per capita* energy consumption levels for 1960 and 1984. As an illustration, for the world as a whole, energy consumption would have risen 46 per cent between 1960 and 1984 had the world's population in 1984 consumed energy at the 1960 *per capita* level. Thus 46 per cent of the growth in energy consumption was "due to" population growth, and 54 per cent, the remainder, to rising *per capita* consumption levels – i.e. economic growth. Asia shows a marked increase because of rising standards of living, and this is revealed also in the *per capita* consumption levels. Overall, then, population growth certainly has significant impacts on non-renewable resources, typified here by energy. But rising income levels account for slightly more of the growing world energy consumption than does population growth. Rising income levels are seen to be especially important in explaining energy consumption growth in Asia and Europe.

(c) Renewable Resources
Population growth has unquestionably had impacts upon renewable resource availability. Until the Second World War, agricultural output expansion was mainly met from expanding the area under cultivation. Box 7.5 shows broad estimates of changes in land use for the world's major regions between 1850 and 1980. The picture is systematic. Only in Europe has cropland area remained static (and will in fact decline as agricultural price support schemes are phased out). This expansion has been at the cost of losses in forest land, wetlands and grassland.

Box 7.5 World Land Use Change by Region, 1850–1980

| | % change in area 1850–1980 | | |
	Forests	Grassland	Cropland
All Regions:	−15	− 1	+179
Tropical Africa	−20	+ 9	+288
Latin America	−19	−23	+677
North America	− 3	−22	+309
China	−39	− 3	+ 79
S Asia	−43	− 1	+196
SE Asia	− 7	−25	+670
Europe	+ 4	+ 8	− 4
USSR	−12	− 1	+147

Source: IIED and World Resources Institute, *World Resources 1987*, Basic Books, New York, 1987, p. 272.

The links between deforestation and population growth have been investigated in several studies. A Finnish study[14] produced an extensive statistical test of the factors influencing deforestation in seventy-two tropical countries. They related a measure of deforestation in a given year to indicators of soil-erosion sensitivity, climate, accessibility of the forest area, extent of shifting cultivation and grazing, extent of fuelwood collection, various indicators of economic development, land tenure and population pressure. Forest coverage was found to be very closely correlated with population density and population growth rates in all countries except eight arid African countries. Food production was also correlated with deforestation, indicating that increased food output has been secured by forest clearance for agricultural land use. To a limited extent, income *per capita* was also correlated with deforestation. Using the statistical relationships, the authors project levels of deforestation up to the year 2025 under various assumptions. The general result is that very large-scale deforestation can be expected in the future, particularly in Latin America.

The Finnish study related to a single year (1980) and the analysis was therefore based on "cross-sectional" data – i.e. data for different countries but at the same point in time. It did not contain any price variables that might explain deforestation – e.g. timber export prices. Another study found that population was relatively *unimportant* as an explanation of deforestation when compared to other factors such as income, agricultural self-sufficiency, currency devaluation and arable land *per capita*.[15] That study used time-series but, in the absence of annual deforestation data, used logging rates as a proxy. This may be unsatisfactory if logging is itself not well correlated with deforestation generally. Moreover, one would expect price variables to be more relevant when logging is the change that is being explained, since logging will be responsive to market conditions.

One other statistical study of deforestation attempted to link population growth to deforestation, allowing for linkages between population change and agriculture.[16] This study used "panel" data (a mix of time-series and cross-sectional data) for

1968–72, and the models linked deforestation (measured by the annual change in forest area), population growth or population density, the change in cultivated land area, growth in GNP, and the change in woodfuels production and roundwood export. The results were that:

> population change was a significant explanatory variable of changes in forest area, more so in Africa and Asia than in Latin America;
> the expansion of arable land is associated with forest loss, and is related to population growth;
> GNP is not associated with reductions in forest area, nor is *per capita* wood production;
> in the longer term, deforestation is more prevalent in those countries where there is a high level of wood use (woodfuels or wood export), i.e. deforestation is related to the past level of wood use.

Clearly, the studies are not wholly in accord on how population change impacts on deforestation. Those that use direct measures of deforestation, themselves subject to significant margins of error, tend to support a direct population–deforestation linkage. Those that use logging rates as proxies for deforestation suggest that price variations and GNP are important, and population is relatively unimportant. These studies illustrate just how complex the interactive process is between population and the environment.

Land tenure itself is frequently important in this context, as a study in Ecuador shows.[17] A simple Malthusian hypothesis linking deforestation with population pressure was rejected because the areas under study exhibited no secular increase in population density between 1974 and 1982, the period covered by the study. Land and resource tenure arrangements contribute strongly, since land claims can be adjudicated only if at least half of any settled land is cleared of vegetation. Fallow lands can also be claimed by agricultural colonists, deterring existing fallow arrangements which maintained much of the land under forest cover. Logging concessions were banned in 1982, placing the burden of supplying timber on colonists who depleted the forests inefficiently. The growth in their activity is revealed by the rapid increase in the import of chainsaws. The Ecuadorian government has also banned log exports; this has had the effect of keeping timber prices low, in turn discouraging any afforestation effort. Forest protection is also severely limited by the lack of forest rangers and low expenditure on research and extension. The studies link the extent of deforestation to the extent of agricultural colonization and an index of the extent to which formal land tenure is held. Land clearance was found to be affected by both population pressure and tenurial arrangements.[18] Simple relationships between population growth and renewable resource loss therefore tend to conceal the myriad factors contributing to resource degradation.

(d) Common property
Resources that have no owners are known as "open access" resources. The atmosphere and large parts of the world's oceans would be examples. Resources that are owned by a community (village, tribe, nation, etc.) are known as "common property". It is widely argued that open access resources are at risk of extinction because no individual has an incentive to conserve the resource – this is the true "tragedy of the commons".[19] Common property resources may be well managed: this will depend on the controls exercised by the society owning the resource.

Population growth contributes to the overuse of common property and open access resources, be it rangelands, the world's oceans, or the atmosphere. Atmospheric trace gases contributing to the "greenhouse effect" are strongly linked to energy consumption which, in turn, is linked partly to population growth, as we have seen.

In the oceans it is now widely recognized that most fisheries are fully exploited, and a number are seriously overfished. Box 7.6 shows total catches by the major fishing nations between 1962 and 1986. The data are not totally reliable owing to under-reporting of catches in a number of countries, but the trends are clear: fish catches increased dramatically until about 1970, after which the growth rate slowed, partly because of overfishing

Box 7.6   **Fish Catches for Major Fishing Nations, 1962–1986**

| | *(million tonnes: freshwater plus marine)* | | | |
	1962	1972	1982	1984/86
World	45.7	62.3	76.5	86.9
USA	2.9	2.8	4.1	4.8
Canada	1.2	1.1	1.4	1.4
Japan	6.8	9.9	11.0	11.8
China	4.1	3.7	5.1	6.9
India	1.0	1.8	2.4	2.9
Indonesia	0.9	1.3	2.1	2.4
Korea (S)	0.5	1.3	2.3	2.7
Thailand	0.4	1.7	2.2	2.2
Norway	1.4	3.0	2.7	2.2
UK	1.0	1.1	0.9	0.9
USSR	3.8	8.2	9.9	10.8
Chile	0.7	0.7	3.8	5.0
Peru	7.1	3.5	2.5	4.4

Source: United Nations Environment Programme, *Environmental Data Report*, Blackwell, Oxford, 1987, and second edition 1989/90, Oxford, 1990.

which, in turn, is due to demand induced by population growth, and to income growth. The figures for Norway and the United Kingdom illustrate the decline in the Atlantic herring and cod industry. Total catches of Atlantic cod have fallen from around 1.5 million tonnes in 1965 to about 600,000 tonnes in the 1980s. The haddock catch has fallen from 250,000 tonnes to just over 50,000 tonnes.

There is a complex link between population change and common property resources, where common property relates to resources that are "owned" and managed by a community. Traditional communal systems did tend to regulate the use rate of resources, and many such resources – for example, Swiss mountain resources or Japanese village commons – are effectively managed this way today.[20] Indeed, there is even some evidence to suggest that communal management emerges in its strongest form where environments are most fragile, but the relationship is far from unambiguous. There is some evidence to suggest further that population growth was itself managed so as to keep within the carrying capacity of natural environments, or, where population growth occurred, technological response took place so as to raise food output per hectare. Common property systems have declined for many reasons, including population growth. Other factors include colonialism as a destroying force, acquisition of the resources by national governments (70–80 per cent of tropical forests, for example, are state-owned), and the setting of ecologically unsound price signals through subsidies to deforestation, irrigation, etc.

(e) Urban pollution and congestion

The rapid growth of urban populations clearly results in squalor, slums and ill-health. Unable to afford land in the town or city, poor households occupy the urban margins, invariably without sanitation or clean water supplies. Around 4 billion people are expected to be crowded into the world's urban centres by 2025. Each year adds 50 million extra urban dwellers.[21] The extent of overcrowding can be partially gauged by comparing population densities for major cities in the developing world with those for the developed world. Chicago has around 2500 people per square kilometre, Philadelphia has some 3000. London has 4000 and Milan about 9000. Cairo has 24,000, Casablanca 12,000, Buenos Aires 15,000, Santiago 17,000, Lima 29,000. But top of the league are Mexico City, with 34,000 people per square kilometre, Manila, with 43,000, and Calcutta, with 88,000. Despite these concentrations, progress is being made with connections to water supply and sanitation. Air pollution has increased dramatically in many urban congested areas, although data for the developing world are very limited. São Paulo has shown an increase in sulphur oxides concentration but a decrease in particulate (smoke) concentration, reflecting a policy of trying to combat the more visible pollutant. Manila, on the other hand, has reduced sulphur oxides but increased particulates.[22] Clearly, trends in air pollution are determined as much by policy measures and the nature of the urban economy as by population density.

Box 7.7   **Prevalence of Energy-deficient Diets in 87 Developing Countries, 1980**

Country group or region	Not enough calories for an active working life (below 90 per cent of FAO/WHO requirement)		Not enough calories to prevent stunted growth and serious health risks (below 80 per cent of FAO/WHO requirement)	
	Share in population (per cent)	Population (millions)	Share in population (per cent)	Population (millions)
Developing countries (87)	34	730	16	340
Low-income (30)	51	590	23	270
Middle-income (57)	14	140	7	70
Sub-Saharan Africa (37)	44	150	25	90
East Asia and Pacific (8)	14	40	7	20
South Asia (7)	50	470	21	200
Middle East and North Africa (11)	10	20	4	10
Latin America and the Caribbean (24)	13	50	6	20

Note: Bracketed number refers to number of countries in the group.
Source: World Bank, *Poverty and Hunger*, World Bank, Washington, DC, 1986, p. 17.

Population and Poverty

The measurement of poverty has attracted a significant literature of its own.[23] Certainly, income *per capita* is one of the factors in poverty. A widely used measure of poverty is based on the incidence of energy-deficient diets. Two measures relate to the extent to which the population is below a standard of either (a) the calories needed to prevent stunted growth and serious health risks, or (b) the calories needed for an active working life. Box 7.7 shows broad estimates of the numbers of people falling into these categories. The narrower definition would place some 340 million people "below the poverty line", and the wider one some 730 million (China is excluded). Maybe 40 per cent of the poor are children under ten; 75 per cent live in rural areas; some 80 per cent of the income of the poor is spent on food, often with very little meat; most are malnourished; most are susceptible to diseases. Of every ten children born to poor parents, two die within a year, another dies before the age of five, and only five survive beyond the age of forty.[24]

As far as diet is concerned, the problem is not the global *availability* of food but *access* to food. The world's food production has actually outstripped the world's population growth. In Sub-Saharan Africa, *per capita* food production has actually fallen. In general, the problem of energy-deficient diets is one of access, or *food security*, and food security is in considerable part a problem of inadequate purchasing power.[25]

The link between poverty and environmental degradation may be further investigated by asking *where* the poor are located. The geographical distribution is shown in Box 7.8. *Within* these regions the notable feature is that the poor are located in (a) ecologically fragile rural locations and (b) the peripheries of cities, frequently themselves fragile living areas. "Fragility" here relates to the low resilience of the areas to stress or shocks such as climatic variation or population pressure. It is the relationship between this resilience, or lack of it, and the demands made on natural resources that matters. Thus parts of Western Europe, the "corn belt" of the USA, the Nile Delta,

Box 7.8   **Geographical Location of the World's Poor**

Region	Millions of People	Percentage of:	
		Region's Population	Poorest People in Developing Countries
S Asia	350	33%	50%
China	76	7%	11%
E Asia	31	6%	4%
Africa (Sub-Saharan)	137	26%	20%
Near East + N Africa	34	13%	5%
Latin America	72	16%	10%
Total	700	18%	100%

Source: J. Leonard, *Environment and the Poor: Development Strategies for a Common Agenda*, Transaction Books, New Brunswick for the Overseas Development Council, Washington, DC, 1989.

the Ganges floodplain and the intensive rice-growing areas of South-East Asia have stable climates, alluvial soils and support very large populations with reasonably limited environmental problems.

Ecologically fragile environments are typified by tropical forests, where soils are acidic and subject to serious erosion once deforestation occurs; upland areas where soil erosion is a serious risk; and arid and semi-arid zones where soils are light and easily eroded by wind.

Of the 700 million poor people recorded in Box 7.8, it is estimated that 250 million live in areas where it is feasible to intensify agriculture through the application of fertilizers and modern technology. In this sense any fragility in the ecosystem is capable of substitution by capital inputs. Some 350 million people live in areas where such substitution generally is either much more difficult or unfeasible because of climatic and poor soil conditions. The remaining 100 million people in the poorest groups live in the peripheral urban areas which in turn are often high-risk areas because of landslides, floods, lack of sanitation and lack of infrastructure. It is these 450 million people in the low productive-potential areas and the urban margins who constitute the *marginalized poor*.[26]

Policy on Population and Environment

The evidence indicates that population growth has two broadly counteracting impacts on environment and development. By "forcing" adaptive and technological change, population growth may actually increase the prospects for development in the traditional sense of rising GNP *per capita*. By contributing to the depletion of natural resources – primarily the renewable open access and common property natural resources – population growth impedes development in the traditional sense and certainly reduces environmental quality. The balance of these two broad impacts favours the view that population growth, at least on the scale now being witnessed, is detrimental to future human welfare.[27] Such growth threatens both the quantity and the quality of natural resources, including the waste-assimilative capacities of the environment. Moreover, to argue that population growth can be associated with advances in technology does not mean that technological advance will not occur without population change. Such a view overlooks the extent to which conscious decisions to invest in new technology can be made for reasons unassociated with the need to feed, house and supply with energy an increasing number of people.

But reducing population growth rates will contribute only partly to solving environmental problems. Many other factors generate resource degradation, especially misdirected policies concerning land tenure and prices, whilst poverty functions in a "disabling" role. Major advances can be made by reforming government policy which directly or indirectly affects environmental quality. China, for example, has increased agricultural output and reduced poverty dramatically by improving farmers' incentives and placing land under household management.[28] Malawi has increased agricultural output by 7 per cent per annum since 1973, despite having the third highest rural population density in Africa. The potential for energy conservation is substantial in both developed and developing world alike. Proper pricing and proper incentives offer the scope for substantial resource conservation.[29] But policies must be advanced on many fronts, and these must include major additional efforts to control birth rates – especially in Sub-Saharan Africa, where the traditional model of population control appears not to be working. Population policy in turn requires not just investment in information about the benefits of reduced family size, and about contraception, but also a major effort to understand and modify the underlying cultural factors which continue to favour the large family. Ultimately, development will stabilize populations, but in many cases development itself is threatened by over-rapid population growth.

Notes

1. See World Bank, *World Development Report 1984*, World Bank, Washington, DC, 1985, p. 69.
2. The fertility rate is a measure of the number of births per individual (or a group or a population). Broadly speaking, therefore, it is the number of children actually born to a woman of childbearing age.
3. Sub-Saharan Africa relates to Africa other than Morocco, Tunisia, Libya, Algeria, Western Sahara, Egypt and South Africa.
4. A population's "doubling time", t, is given by the equation $e^{xt} = 2$, where x is the growth rate.
5. See World Bank, *Population Growth and Policies in Sub-Saharan Africa*, Washington, DC, 1986.
6. See Food and Agriculture Organization, *Potential Population Supporting Capacities of Lands in the Developing World*, FAO, Rome, Report FPA/INT/513, 1982. For a popular version see FAO, *Land, Food and People*, FAO Economic and Social Development Series No. 30, Rome, 1984.
7. D. Steeds, *Desertification in the Sahelian and Sudanian Zones of West Africa*, World Bank, Washington, DC, 1985.
8. Important works establishing this linkage are E. Boserup, *The Conditions of Agricultural Growth*, Aldine, Chicago; *Population and Technological Change*, University of Chicago Press, Chicago, 1981; and P. L. Pingali and H. Binswanger, "Population Density and Agricultural Intensification: A Study of the Evolution of

Technologies in Tropical Agriculture", Report ARU 22, Agriculture and Rural Development Department, World Bank, 1984.

9. See H. Ruthenberg, *Farming Systems in the Tropics*, 3rd edn, Oxford University Press, Oxford, 1980, especially Section 4.5.
10. The estimates here are taken from G. Woodwell, "On the Limits of Nature", in R. Repetto (ed.), *The Global Possible*, Yale University Press, New Haven, 1985, pp. 47–65.
11. See P. Vitousek *et al.*, "Human Appropriation of the Products of Photosynthesis", *Bioscience*, vol. 34, no. 6, 1986, pp. 368–73.
12. See, for example, H. Daly and J. Cobb, *For the Common Good: Redirecting the Economy Toward Community, the Environment and a Sustainable Future*, Beacon Press, Boston, 1989.
13. That is, we compute $e_0/p_0 = p_1$ and subtract from it e_0. The result is then expressed as a percentage of $e_1 - e_0$, where e is total energy consumption, p is population and the subscripts $_1$ and $_0$ are 1984 and 1960 respectively.
14. M. Palo, G. Mery and J. Salmi, "Deforestation in the Tropics: Pilot Scenarios Based on Quantitative Analysis", in M. Palo and J. Salmi, *Deforestation or Development in the Third World?*, Finnish Forest Research Institute, Helsinki, 1987, pp. 53–106.
15. A. Capistrano and C. Kiker, "Global Economic Influences on Tropical Closed Broadleaved Forest Depletion 1967–1985", Food and Resource Economics Department, University of Florida, Gainsville, May 1990, mimeo.
16. See J. Allen and D. Barnes, "The Causes of Deforestation in Developing Countries", *Annals of the Association of American Geographers*, vol. 75, no. 2, 1985, pp. 163–84.
17. D. Southgate "How to Promote Tropical Deforestation: The Case of Ecuador", Department of Agricultural Economics and Rural Sociology, Ohio State University, mimeo, June 1989; and D. Southgate, R. Sierra and L. Brown, "The Causes of Deforestation in Ecuador: A Statistical Analysis", London Environmental Economics Centre, LEEC Paper 89–09, London, 1989.
18. More formally, the model has two equations. The first regresses the size of a canton's agricultural labour force on its non-agricultural labour force, the agricultural productivity of the soil and the extent of a canton's all-weather road network. This equation then "explains" the extent of agricultural colonization. The second equation regresses deforestation on this measure of colonization and on land tenure. Southgate's findings are consistent with other work which explains deforestation in terms of inefficient government interventions such as tax concessions for land clearance, tenure through clearance, log export bans

designed to capture rents for the domestic wood processing industry, etc. See, notably, R. Repetto and M. Gillis, *Public Policies and the Misuse of Forest Resources*, Cambridge University Press, Cambridge, 1988; R. Repetto, *The Forest for the Trees?: Government Policies and the Misuse of Forest Resources*, World Resources Institute, Washington, DC, 1988; H. Binswanger, *Brazilian Policies that Encourage Deforestation in the Amazon*, Environment Department, World Bank, Working Paper No. 16, Washington, DC, April 1989; and D. Mahar, *Government Policies and Deforestation in Brazil's Amazon Region*, Environment Department, World Bank, Working Paper No. 7, Washington, DC, June 1988. For further discussion, see Chapter 9.

19. The term was coined by Garrett Hardin in his "Tragedy of the Commons", *Science*, vol. 162, 13 December 1968, pp. 1243–8. But what Hardin was in fact writing about was open access resources, not common property.

20. See R. Repetto and T. Holmes, "The Role of Population in Resource Depletion in Developing Countries", *Population and Development Review*, vol. 9, no. 4, December 1983, pp. 609–32.

21. See United Nations Centre for Human Settlements, *Global Report on Human Settlements 1986*, Oxford University Press, Oxford, 1987, p. 51.

22. See World Health Organization, *Urban Air Pollution 1973–1980*, WHO, Geneva, 1984.

23. For a survey, see A. B. Atkinson, "Poverty", in J. Eatwell *et al.*, *The New Palgrave: A Dictionary of Economics*, Macmillan, London, 1987.

24. World Bank, *World Development Report 1980*, Oxford University Press, Oxford, 1980.

25. See World Bank, *Poverty and Hunger: Issues and Options for Food Security in Developing Countries*, World Bank, Washington, DC, 1986. The idea that access to food, or goods in general, is the problem is developed in the context of famines by A. Sen, *Poverty and Famine: An essay on Entitlement and Deprivation*, Oxford University Press, Oxford, 1981.

26. See J. Leonard, *Environment and the Poor: Development Strategies for a Common Agenda*, Transaction Books, New Brunswick, 1989.

27. For a strongly optimistic view which argues that population growth is almost systematically beneficial see J. Simon, *Theory of Population and Economic Growth*, Blackwell, Oxford, 1986. Simon's views are partly an extension of the population–technological progress argument presented in this chapter. He also

argues that the greater the supply of people, the more chance there is of finding inventors and scientists whose discoveries will increase long-run human welfare. He omits to note that the same argument could be applied to the supply of individuals whose actions materially diminish human welfare – e.g. a Hitler or a Stalin.

28. For a general discussion see R. Repetto, "Population, Resources, Environment: An Uncertain Future", *Population Bulletin*, vol. 42, no. 2, 1987.

29. These issues are discussed at length in D. W. Pearce and J. Warford, *Environment and Economic Development: Managing Natural Resources in the Developing World*, forthcoming, 1991.

8

Tropical Deforestation

Ed Barbier

Current arguments over the state of the world's tropical forests appear to be polarized between *preservation* and *development* views. There is a growing awareness, particularly in industrialized nations, of tropical forests as "unique" ecosystems, a major source of the world's biological diversity with important climatic functions – notably their role in global warming as an important "store" of carbon. At its extreme, this argument calls for complete *preservation* of the tropical forests, with no human use permitted at all, except perhaps by communities of forest-dwellers who have traditionally used and managed the natural forests in a sustainable manner. However, many people within tropical forest countries see the forests and the land they cover as resources that should be exploited for economic *development*. Forest lands are therefore seen as valuable sources of commercial timber, or as land for agriculture and mining. The emphasis is on "opening up" the forest, through road-building and infrastructure investments, and "developing" forest resources, through building hydro-electric dams, establishing timber concessions, encouraging agricultural development and allowing shifting cultivation as a "release valve" for population pressure.

To the extent that these *development* options allow little regeneration of the natural forests and are essentially irreversible, significant destruction of the tropical forest ecosystems will occur. This does not need to happen. There is a variety of *conservation* or "natural management" options which maintain the tropical forest system in broadly its original state while at the same time allowing important human uses of forest resources. For example, limited selective logging might be permitted with subsequent natural or managed regeneration of the removed timber. Non-timber products, such as latex, rattan, honey and resins, can be harvested without destruction of the forest system. "Shifting cultivation" and other agricultural practices could be implemented with full-regeneration rotations.

In short, there are numerous land-use options for tropical forests. Preservation, conservation or development should not be completely dismissed. They all have their role to play in ensuring overall sustainable development of tropical forest lands. Even some clear-felling of timber without regeneration or wholesale conversion of forest land may be justified if all the costs of the irreversible loss of tropical forest resources and ecological functions are properly accounted for and considered less significant than the gains from these developments.

Unfortunately, it is rare that either of these conditions is met. Many functions and resources of natural/managed tropical forest systems yield values that are *non-marketed* (e.g. watershed protection, subsistence products, habitat conservation, future uses, etc.). In contrast, many development options yield *marketed* products – such as timber, crops, minerals, meat, hydroelectricity – that have commercial value. Choice of land use may therefore be biased towards too much conversion and overexploitation of forest and too little natural management of forest land.

Thus any economic analysis of tropical deforestation must first be concerned with the *total economic value*, both marketed and non-marketed, that is being surrendered through modifications to prevailing natural/managed forest systems. The crucial policy issue is the correction of any imbalances or distortions in *incentives* that allow tropical forests to be converted or exploited without taking full account of the market and non-market values that are being forgone. Doing this may require first demonstrating to governments and international agencies, in both developing and industrialized countries, that tropical forests have economic values when they are conserved and utilized sustainably. Finally, a substantial part of the total economic value of tropical forests may accrue to nations other than those containing them. In particular, the carbon store value of the forest and its unique biological diversity have global value. Some means of *international transfers* must therefore be devised to allow nations to pay tropical forest countries for conserving these values.

Extent of Deforestation

The main concern with tropical deforestation is over the state of the closed broadleaved (hardwood) forests in developing countries. The rainforests – or tropical "moist" forests (TMF), as they are usually called – are the most expansive (see Box 8.1). They cover 1046 million hectares, around 9 per cent of earth's total land area, and comprise about 80 per cent of all remaining tropical closed forests. Over half of this TMF area is in Latin America; the rest is shared about equally between Africa and the Asian Pacific. Approximately 91 per cent of the world's remaining tropical moist forests is concentrated in Amazonia, Central Africa and the South-East Asian islands (including Malaysia), totalling around 950 million hectares (ha), or roughly the area of China. Brazil has the single largest TMF area, at 347 million ha, three times the forest area of Indonesia or Zaïre. Together these three countries make up 45 per cent of the total TMF area.

Estimates of tropical forest deforestation have varied widely. The most recent estimates by the United Nations Food and Agricultural Organization (FAO), reported in Box 8.1, indicate that by the end of the 1980s the annual rate of TMF deforestation was well over 8.4 million ha. Over one-third of this deforestation is occurring in Brazil alone. However, other estimates of the rate of deforestation in Brazil have put the figures between 5 and 8 million ha, which increases global annual tropical deforestation to as much as 14 to 15 million ha.

Estimating the extent of tropical deforestation in developing countries is not an easy task. The main interest has been in the loss of *broadleaved closed forests*. The FAO defines these as stands of broadleaved (hardwood) forests, which have sufficient canopy to cover a large area of ground (40 per cent crown cover or more), little undergrowth, and are

Box 8.1 **Deforestation in Tropical Countries**

Estimated Tropical Moist Forest (TMF) Deforestation, 1990

	Total forest area (mn ha)	Undisturbed operable forest (mn ha)	Annual deforesta- tion (000 ha)	Total TMF area deforested (mn ha)
AMAZONIA	613.6	453	4129	100
Brazil	347.0		3200	
Peru	73.0		300	
Bolivia	55.5		60	
Venezuela	42.0		150	
Colombia	41.4		350	
Guyana	19.3		3	
Suriname	15.2		3	
Ecuador	12.3		60	
Fr. Guyana	7.9		3	
CENTRAL AFRICA	167.1	107	325	30
Zaïre	103.8		200	
Congo	21.1		22	
Gabon	20.3		15	
Cameroon	17.1		80	
Cen. Afr. Rep.	3.6		5	
Eq. Guinea	1.2		3	
SE ASIA ISLANDS	167.3	72	1707	117
Indonesia	108.6		1315	
Papua NG	33.5		22	
Malaysia	18.4		255	
Philippines	6.5		110	
Brunei	0.3		5	
Total	948.0	632	6180	247
Other areas	97.7	<20	2300	177
World total	1045.7	652	8480	424

Notes: *Tropical moist forests* include wetland and mangrove forests but exclude the deciduous dry forests of South Asia, Sub-Saharan Africa and sub-tropical South America. In 1988, the FAO estimated the total area of *tropical closed forests* (including deciduous dry forests) to be 1269.6 million ha.
Source: R. Schmidt, "Sustainable Management of Tropical Moist Forests", Presentation for ASEAN Sub-Regional Seminar, Indonesia, Forest Resources Division, Forestry Department, FAO, Rome, January 1990.

often multistoreyed. They may be evergreen, semi-deciduous or deciduous, wet, moist or dry. However, the vast majority of the world's "tropical" broadleaved closed forests are the *tropical moist forests* of Amazonia, Central Africa and the South-East Asian archipelago. Other important closed forests in developing countries include mangroves and other wetland forests and the deciduous dry forests of South Asia, Sub-Saharan Africa and sub-tropical South America.

Although developments in remote sensing and satellite imagery have improved measurement techniques, estimates of tropical deforestation still vary widely. For example, in the 1970s the deforestation rate of tropical closed forests was thought to be around 11–15 million ha. The global forest resources assessment in 1980 by FAO, updated in 1988, indicated that the rate was more likely to be around 7 million ha, with 4 million ha being deforested in Latin America alone. However, these estimates relied heavily on data provided by government forestry departments rather than measurement by satellites and other forms of remote sensing. Alternative estimates on tropical deforestation presented by the World Resources Institute (WRI) and Norman Myers for the mid- and late 1980s suggest a much higher rate of forest loss – around 14 to 15 million ha. A major reason for these discrepancies was a difference in the estimates of deforestation for Brazil (2–3 million ha by the Brazilian government and FAO, as opposed to 5 million ha by Myers, 8 million ha by WRI), as well as for other key tropical forest countries such as India (WRI 1.5 million ha, FAO 0.15 million ha), Burma (WRI 0.68 million ha, FAO 0.1 million ha) and Indonesia (WRI 0.9 million ha, FAO 0.62 million ha).

The most recent FAO estimates are based on the interim 1988 report on global forest resources, where annual deforestation rates estimated by FAO for the tropical moist forests over 1981–5 were projected to 1990, except for Brazil and Indonesia. For these countries, preliminary satellite imagery and remote-sensing results for 1989 were included. The results are presented in Box 8.1.

The important points arising from Box 8.1 are:

- The present total area of the forests in Amazonia, Central Africa and the South-East Asian Islands (including peninsular Malaysia) account for 91 per cent of the world's remaining tropical moist forest, with the Amazon Basin containing 59 per cent of the global total.
- Outside these areas – in Mexico, Central America, the Caribbean, West Africa and continental tropical Asia – 64 per cent of the tropical forests have already been cleared, and 2.3 per cent continues to be lost each year.
- Of individual countries, Brazil accounts for one-third of the global forests and almost 40 per cent of tropical deforestation; Indonesia and Zaïre contain approximately 10 per cent of the world's forests, yet the rate of deforestation in Indonesia (over 15 per cent of the world total) is more than six times that of Zaïre.

Whatever the actual figure for world tropical deforestation, the state of the forests in Amazonia, Central Africa and the South-East Asian islands is a global concern. These three regions contain 91 per cent of the world's remaining tropical moist forest, with Amazonia alone accounting for 59 per cent of TMF area. Their forests are the last depository of unique values – including the vast majority of the world's unexploited tropical hardwoods and biological diversity.

The Economic Value of Tropical Forests

Tropical deforestation is an economic problem because important values are lost, some perhaps irreversibly, when closed forests are "opened up", degraded or cleared. Each choice or *land-use option* for the forest – to leave it standing in its natural state, or to exploit it selectively, e.g. for timber or "minor" (i.e. non-timber) products, or to clear-cut it entirely so that the land can be converted to another use, such as agriculture – has implications in terms of values gained and lost. The decision as to what land-use option to pursue for a given tropical forest area – and ultimately whether current rates of deforestation are "excessive" – can be made only if these gains and losses are properly analysed and evaluated. This requires that *all the values* that are gained and lost with each land-use option are carefully considered.

For example, preserving a tropical forest involves direct costs in terms of setting up a protected area, paying forest guards and rangers to patrol and maintain the area, and perhaps the cost of establishing a "buffer zone" for surrounding local communities. Development options, such as the use of the forest for commercial timber exploitation and of the converted forest land and resources for agriculture, mining and hydroelectricity, are sacrificed if preservation is chosen. These forgone development benefits are additional costs associated with the preservation option. Such costs are easily identifiable, as they often comprise marketable outputs and income sacrificed (e.g. timber revenue, agricultural income, mineral wealth, hydroelectricity). It is not surprising, therefore, that governments and donors usually consider the *total costs* – the direct costs plus the forgone development benefits – of preservation in their choice of land-use options for tropical forests.

But the same approach should be taken in evaluating development options for the forest. For example, if the forest is to be cleared for agriculture, not only should the direct costs of conversion (e.g. clearing and burning, establishing crops) be included as part of the costs of this land-use option, but so must the *forgone* values of the forest that has been converted. These may include both the loss of important *environmental functions* (watershed protection, micro-climate maintenance) and *resources* (commercial hardwoods, non-timber products, wildlife).

In other words, we must determine the *total economic value* (TEV), both marketed and non-marketed, that is being surrendered through modifications of the prevailing forest land-use entailed by any development option. These values comprise direct and indirect *use* values, *option* values and *existence* values (see Box 8.2). Direct use values include timber and non-timber products and ecotourism. Indirect use values are essentially the ecological functions of tropical forests: their watershed protection, micro-climatic and material cycling functions. All

Box 8.2 **Total Economic Value of Tropical Forests and Development Options**

The table indicates the many *use* and *non-use* values of a tropical forest that may comprise its *total economic value* (TEV):

Classification of Total Economic Value for Tropical Forests

	Use Values		Non-Use Values
(1) *Direct Value*	*(2)* *Indirect Value*	*(3)* *Option Value*	*Existence Value*
Sustainable timber products	Nutrient cycling	Future Uses as per (1), (2)	Biodiversity
Non-timber products	Watershed protection		Culture, Heritage
Recreation	Air pollution reduction		
Medicine			
Plant genetics	Micro-climatic functions		
Education	Carbon store		
Human habitat			

Source: D. W. Pearce, *An Economic Approach to Saving the Tropical Forests*, LEEC Paper 90-05, London Environmental Economics Centre, London, 1990.

Direct use values are the resources and "services" provided directly by the forest. *Indirect use values* are essentially the environmental functions of the forest, which indirectly support economic activity and human welfare. *Option value* relates to the amount individuals would be willing to pay to conserve a tropical forest, or at least some of its uses, for future use. Individuals are essentially valuing the guaranteed "option" of future supply of these uses, the availability of which might otherwise be uncertain. *Existence value* relates to valuatiion of the resource as a unique asset in itself, with no connection to its use values. This would include forests as objects of intrinsic and "stewardship" value, as a bequest to future generations, and as a unique cultural and heritage asset.

these values may have an "option value" component if we are interested in preserving them for future use. Finally, existence values are the values that people place on the forest "in itself" and are unrelated to any use.

Calculation of the above components of total economic value is important for assessing the costs and benefits of different forest land-use options. Of crucial importance is the distinction between *preservation*, which would be formally equivalent to outright non-use of the resource; *sustainable conservation (management)*, which would involve limited uses of the forest consistent with leaving the original natural forest and ecosystem broadly intact; and *complete development (conversion)* – e.g. clear-cutting the forest and converting the land to some alternative, agricultural use. In all approaches, the basic *cost-benefit analaysis* (CBA) rule for any pair of alternative land-use options, A and B, is to compare the net benefits of each. That is, as the opportunity cost of choosing option A is forgoing the net benefits of B, it is not enough for the net benefits of A to be positive. The net benefits of A (NB_a) must *exceed* the forgone net benefits of B (NB_b):

$$NB_a - NB_b > 0$$

For example, if the forest is to be cleared for agriculture (option A), not only should the direct costs of conversion (e.g. clearing and burning, establishing crops) be included as part of the costs of this land-use option, but so must the *forgone* values of the forest that has been converted, which would have been preserved in its natural state (option B). These may include both the loss of important *environmental functions* (watershed protection, micro-climatic maintenance) and *resources* (commercial hardwoods, non-timber products, wildlife) that comprise important use and non-use values.

Calculating the components of TEV is therefore essential to applying the above cost-benefit analysis (CBA) rule to the various land-use options proposed for tropical forest development. However, care should be taken in adding up the various components of TEV, as there are inevitable trade-offs among them.

Furthermore, a measure of TEV is in itself not enough to justify any sustainable management regime – even one that achieves maximum TEV. Such a measure does not tell us anything about the opportunity costs – the next best land-use option forgone – of the sustainable management regime. By applying the above CBA rule it is possible to determine which development option should take place.

However, many of the component values in total economic value have no market – especially subsistence or underdeveloped non-timber products and the indirect use, option and existence values of forests. Choice of land use is therefore often *biased* in favour of land uses that do have marketed outputs – e.g. development options such as ranching, timber exploitation, agriculture, mining, hydroelectricity. The result is too much conversion and overexploitation of forest and too little natural management of forest land.

The basic reason for the imbalance is that the non-market values of the natural/managed systems are not automatically reflected in the price of forested land. For example, the market value of land converted to agriculture fails to reflect the lost environmental benefits, such as watershed protection. If "owners" (i.e. those with legal title and those who have acquired the land on a first-come basis) had to pay the full social cost of developing forested land, less land would be converted or overexploited. Forested land is clearly *underpriced*. An important consequence is that once the land occupied has become sufficiently degraded and thus significantly less productive, the "owners" have a strong incentive to abandon it for new, virgin forested land which is "cheap" to acquire and develop. The process repeats itself until it becomes difficult to get access to new forest lands – for example because of the lack of roads or waterways into a region.

There is clearly a role for government in ensuring that the total economic value of forest land lost through conversion and exploitation is accounted for as part of the costs of these development options. This suggests a policy of:

carrying out *cost-benefit analysis* (CBA) *of land-use options*, where the CBA takes as full account as possible of both market and non-market values. For example, the environmental functions of forests must be fully evaluated;

lowering the *incentives to exploit "new" land* so that a better pattern of land uses is secured; and

improving the *incentives to stay on/restore degraded land* by raising productivity of that land.

Cost and Benefits of Forest Land-Use Options

If proper economic valuation of forest losses takes place, the cost of forest conversion and degradation can often be high. For example, in Indonesia, the forgone cost in terms of timber rentals from converting primary and secondary forest land is in the order of US$625–750 million per annum. With logging damage and fire accounting for additional costs of US$70 million, this would represent losses of around US$800 million annually. The inclusion of forgone non-timber products would raise this cost to US$1 billion per year. In addition, the loss of timber on sites used for development projects could be another US$40–100 million (Pearce, Barbier and Markandya, 1990, ch. 5). The total cost of the depreciation of the forest stock would include not just the cost of conversion but also the cost of timber extraction and forest degradation. One study estimated this total cost for Indonesia to be around US$3.1 billion in 1982, or approximately 4 per cent of GDP (Repetto *et al.*, 1987). However, this estimate must be considered a lower bound, as it does not include the value of the loss of forest protection functions (watershed protection, micro-climatic maintenance) and of biodiversity. The latter may be particularly important in terms of *option and existence values* – i.e. values reflecting a willingness to pay to see species conserved for future use or for their intrinsic worth – which could translate into future payments that the rest of the world might make to Indonesia to conserve forest lands. Similar arguments apply to the value of the forest as a *carbon store*.

A common assumption is that the values of tropical forests

that are very difficult to quantify must be less significant. This may not be true. For example, Pearce (1990) has shown how the existence value of the Amazonian tropical forests may easily dominate its direct and indirect use values. On the assumption that the Amazon forest is valued at an average of US$8 per adult in the advanced economies of the world (only), existence value would total US$3.2 billion, or a quarter of the entire GDP contribution of Amazonia to the Brazilian economy, inclusive of mineral extraction, timber and agriculture. If this money was collected from individuals in the advanced economies and placed in an "Amazon Conservation Fund", it could be used to compensate those people in the Amazon, contributing to more than 25 per cent of its economic output for "ceasing" their activities.

Additionally, tropical forests could be given "carbon credits" for their role in averting global warming. In this case, the benefit of conserving existing forests would relate to the avoided damage of *not* releasing the stored greenhouse gases (mainly carbon) through deforestation. Pearce (1990) estimates that the value of this function may amount to around US$1300 per ha for a single year, with perhaps similar benefits for about five years. For newly forested areas, values might be of the order of US$130 per ha per annum. Again, provided adequate collection and transfer mechanisms could be found, such "carbon credits" would be a powerful incentive for promoting conservation over development and deforestation.

There is also increasing realization that development options for forest lands do not have to entail substantial deforestation or forest degradation. Timber exploitation is an illustrative example. Logging for timber *can* be consistent with conservation if the timber management regime practises sustainable forestry – i.e. *natural forest management for sustained timber production*. For instance, selective cutting combined with natural regeneration will leave the original forest ecosystem broadly intact. However, a detailed survey of tropical moist forest management systems concluded that only 0.1 per cent of the 828 million ha of

Box 8.3 **The Comparative Economics of Natural Forest Management**

The table shows estimates of the discounted financial returns to six different timber regimes in Indonesia. TPI is the ideal selective cutting system where minimum disruption to the natural forest ecosystem occurs – one type of natural management regime. CHR is "complete harvesting and regeneration", i.e. harvesting of all marketable trees followed by natural regeneration and possibly enrichment planting. INTD involves establishing intensively managed dipterocarp plantations on already cleared land. PULP is the establishment of fast-growing tree plantation for pulp, whereas SAW10/20 refers to saw timber plantations with ten- and twenty-year rotations respectively.

Comparative Financial Profitability of Timber Regimes, Indonesia
(Net Present Value, 1986 US$/ha)

	Discount rate		
Regime	*5%*	*6%*	*10%*
TPI	2705	2409	2177
CHR	2690	2593	2553
INTD		2746	2203
PULP		2926	2562
SAW20		2419	2278
SAW10		2165	2130

Source: D. W. Pearce, *An Economic Approach to Saving the Tropical Forests*, LEEC Paper 90-05, London Environmental Economics Centre, London, 1990. Calculated from data in R. Sedjo, *The Economics of Natural Plantation Forests in Indonesia*, Resources for the Future, Washington, DC, August 1987.

The table confirms that, on purely financial grounds, the natural management regime (TPI) appears less desirable than most plantation systems and clear-cutting systems, unless very low discount rates are applied. However, this may not be the case if the analysis based on *financial* profitability is extended to a full *economic* analysis, i.e. an appraisal of the investment based on its worth to the economy as a whole rather than to the timber concessionaire. The economic appraisal should include non-market economic values, such as a forest's watershed protection functions, any non-timber products, biological diversity and other environmental benefits. On the whole, these values would be greater for natural management rather than clear-cutting or plantation regimes. In addition, although plantations have generally performed well as a source of industrial timber, economic expectations of plantations have often been unrealistic: they are high-risk investments with high up-front costs, are susceptible to pest and disease attacks, and often suffer from mismanagement of forestry budgets. A recent study in Côte d'Ivoire discovered that over a thirty-year period, 1 cubic metre of timber derived from managed natural forest required an investment of US$5.60, whereas 1 cubic metre of timber grown in plantation needed US$7.40.

productive forest is under sustained-yield management (Poore *et al.*, 1989, ch. 9). As indicated in Box 8.3, this bias is again a reflection of appraising natural management systems on the basis of *financial* profitability and not on full *economic* values, aggravated by distortions introduced by government policies. Yet too often the result of unsustainable logging practices and short-cutting cycles is unnecessary, premature depletion of timber concessions. The "opening up" of new forests by concessionaires seeking quick profits may also allow encroachment into these areas of slash-and-burn shifting cultivation and other destructive activities (Repetto, 1990).

Many potential timber revenues are also lost through wasteful forest-clearing. For example, in the Ivory Coast, where 85 per cent of the original tropical moist forest has disappeared, 200 million cubic metres of merchantable timber have been burned over the last twenty-five years during unplanned land-clearing operations. In Ghana, where 80 per cent of the TMF has been removed, only 15 per cent of forest lands were properly exploited for timber before they were converted to other uses (Poore *et al.*, 1989, ch. 3). Similarly, in Brazil, of the estimated 349 million ha of closed hardwood forest in 1985, about 280 million ha were thought to be potentially exploitable for commercial timber. However, only 13.5 million ha were being selectively logged, whereas the TMF area lost through deforestation totalled 25 million ha – nearly twice as much area (Schmidt, 1989). Thus Brazil's annual sawnwood exports of 1 million cubic metres, valued at US$340 million, could possibly have been doubled or tripled if valuable timber had been saved.

The potential economic losses in terms of non-timber products such as essential oils, honey, wildlife products, resins, bamboos, fruits and nuts from deforestation may also be significant. For example, in Indonesia, exports of non-timber products rose from US$17 million in 1973 to US$154 million in 1985, comprising 12 per cent of export earnings. Exports of rattan alone were US$80 million in 1985 (Pearce, Barbier and Markandya, 1990, ch. 5). However, the commercial potential of many non-timber products may be currently underexploited.

The forgone future value of these products may therefore be much higher than their present value. Moreover, many of the important economic uses of non-timber products – for example the use of "wild" forest foods to supplement food security and meet subsistence needs – are non-market and are not often properly accounted for. Consequently, both the forgone commercial and non-market benefits of non-timber products must be incorporated into any assessment of the costs of deforestation. Box 8.4 shows the results of one study of alternative forest land use.

Although the analysis shows that the discounted returns to non-timber products – in this case fruits and latex – compare highly favourably with other land-use options of clear-cutting timber and forest conversion, the results must be interpreted with caution. First, the financial returns to fruit and latex are the *potential returns*. Whether *actual returns*

Box 8.4   The Economic Role of Non-timber Products

A study of rainforest revenues in Peru calculated the comparative financial returns from non-timber products compared to other commercial uses of the same forest:

Financial Returns to Non-Timber Products and Other Forest Uses, in one ha of Forest at Mishana, Rio Nanay, Peru

(Net Present Value, us\$/ha 1989, 5% Discount Rate)

1.	Non-timber harvesting fruit and latex	6330
2.	Sustainable timber harvesting periodic selective cutting	490
Total natural forest value (1. + 2.)		*6820*
3.	Clear-cutting timber harvesting	1001
4.	Plantation harvesting timber and pulpwood[1]	3184
5.	Cattle ranching[2]	2960

Notes: 1. 1.0 ha plantation of *Gmelina aborea* in Brazilian Amazon
2. Gross revenues/ha of fully stocked cattle pastures in Brazilian Amazon, costs of weeding and fencing and animal care not deducted.
Source: C. Peters, A. Gentry and R. Mendelsohn, "Valuation of an Amazonian Rainforest", *Nature*, vol. 339, 29 June 1989, pp. 655–6.

will reach this magnitude is uncertain, as the marketing, post-harvesting processing and exporting prospects necessary for establishing new non-timber products generally is. Indeed, this is precisely an area where government and aid assistance is critically required. Second, the particular hectare of forest studied is near a village 30 kilometres from the Iquitos, with town market prices used for the financial valuation. It may be misleading to extrapolate from this example for the whole tropical rainforest area. Finally, fruit harvesting in Amazon can be destructive, especially to palms. Certain techniques of rubber-tapping, such as "slaughter tapping", have also been known to cause severe tree damage. In general, the record for harvesting non-timber forest products for commercial exploitation is not good, especially where harvesting is potentially destructive, as in the case of tree barks and gum.

On the other hand, the economic role of non-timber products, especially forest foods, in subsistence agriculture may be currently underestimated. They are widely consumed in most rural communities throughout the developing world, and in some cases even in urban areas. They are often important as dietary supplements, as seasonal supplements – most often when cultivated food supplies are in short supply at the end of the crop season – and as emergency supplies during wars and famines. These economic values attributed to forest foods, although difficult to measure, may be very significant.

Box 8.5 illustrates the type of comprehensive cost-benefit analysis required for tropical forest land-use options, taking the example of the Korup Project, Cameroon. Although this example is of a *conservation* rather than a *development* option, the approach is essentially the same. Thus the net benefits of the Korup protected area and project in terms of sustained forest and susbsistence use, tourism, genetic value, watershed protection, control of flooding and soil maintenance, all compare favourably with the opportunity costs of forestry and other development options, generating a substantial overall net benefit to Cameroon.

Box 8.5   Cost-benefit Analysis of Land Use: Korup Project, Cameroon

The Korup Project is an ongoing programme to promote conservation of the rainforest in Korup National Park in Southwest Province, Cameroon. A social cost-benefit analysis (CBA) of the Project undertaken on behalf of the government of Cameroon and World Wide Fund for Nature – UK yielded the following results:

Base Case Result
(NPV £000, 8% Discount Rate)

Direct Costs of Conservation		−11,913
Opportunity Costs		− 3326
Lost stumpage value	− 706	
Lost forest use	−2620	
Direct Benefits		11,995
Sustained forest use	3291	
Replaced subsistence production	977	
Tourism	1360	
Genetic value	481	
Wastershed protection of fisheries	3776	
Control of flood risk	1578	
Soil fertility maintenance	532	
Induced Benefits		4328
Agricultural productivity gain	905	
Induced forestry	207	
Induced cash crops	3216	
Net Benefit – Project		1084
Adjustments		6,462
External trade credit	7246	
Uncaptured genetic value	− 433	
Uncaptured watershed benefits	− 351	
Net Benefit – Cameroon		7545

Source: H. J. Ruitenbeek, *Social Cost-Benefit Analysis of the Korup Project, Cameroon*, Prepared for the World Wide Fund for Nature and the Republic of Cameroon, London, 1989.

Box 8.5 **Continued**

The CBA includes not only the *direct* operating and capital costs of the Project but also the *opportunity costs* of lost timber earnings (lost stumpage value) and lost production from the six resettled villages (lost forest use). Against this must be weighed the *direct benefits* of the Project in the form of sustained forest use beyond the year 2010, when the forest would otherwise have disappeared, replacement subsistence production of the resettled villagers, tourism, minimum expected genetic value of the forest resources in terms of pharmaceuticals, chemicals, agricultural crop improvements, etc., and environmental functions – watershed protection of fisheries, control of flooding and soil fertility maintenance. Also included are *induced benefits*, agricultural and forestry benefits of the Project's development initiatives in the buffer zone. The external trade credit shows a positive benefit to Cameroon of direct external funding of the Project. "Uncaptured genetic value" is a negative adjustment reflecting the fact that Cameroon will be able to capture only 10 per cent of the genetic value through the licensing structures and institutions which it has in place, and "uncaptured watershed benefits" indicates that some of the watershed protection benefits will flow to Nigeria, not Cameroon.

Thus the analysis indicates that the Korup Project offers substantial net economic benefits as a land-use option, both at project level and to Cameroon as a whole.

Economic Policies and Incentives

There is now sufficient economic evidence linking the tropical deforestation problem to economic policies.[1] Too often, the pricing and economic policies of countries with tropical forests distort the costs of deforestation:

the "prices" determined for tropical timber products or the products derived from converted forest land do not incorporate the lost economic values in terms of forgone timber rentals, forgone minor forest products and other direct uses (e.g. tourism), disrupted forest protection and other ecological functions, and the loss of biological diversity,

---

Box 8.6 **Economic Policies and Deforestation**

Repetto (1990) suggests that a useful way of conceptualizing the way the impacts of government economic and pricing policies affect tropical deforestation is by visualizing a set of "concentric circles" moving outward from the forest:

- at the hub are *policies that directly affect timber and forest management*, i.e. forest revenue structures, tenurial institutions governing privatization of forest land and enforcement of traditional use rights, reforestation incentives, and administration of timber harvesting concessions;
- in the next circle are *policies directly influencing the demand for forest products*, i.e. trade and investment incentives to promote wood-using industries, and energy pricing toward fuelwood substitutes;
- in a third circle are *policies directly affecting extensions of the agricultural frontier and the conversion rate of forest land*, i.e. agricultural credit, tax and pricing incentives for frontier agriculture, including policies affecting the relative price of new forest land, the incentives for cultivation at the intensive as opposed to the extensive margin and the concentration of landholdings, as well as public investments that indirectly spur frontier expansion, such as road-building, and public services, such as agricultural research and extension;
- in the outer circle are *macroeconomic polices that indirectly affect deforestation*, i.e. exchange rate policies affecting tropical forest product exports, policies affecting capital markets that influence investors' time horizons, demographic policies, trade and investment policies affecting labour absorption and rural–urban migration.

Source: R. Repetto, "Macroeconomic Policies and Deforestation", paper prepared for UNU/WIDER Project *The Environment and Emerging Development Issues*, 1990.

including any option or existence values;
even the direct costs of harvesting and converting tropical
forests *are often subsidized and/or distorted*, thus encouraging needless destruction.

As outlined in Box 8.6, a useful way of conceptualizing the impacts of these policies is by visualizing a set of "concentric circles" moving outward from the forest. Much attention has focused on how government economic and pricing policies *directly* affect the costs of deforestation. For example, in the Brazilian Amazon subsidies and other policy distortions are estimated to have accounted for at least 35 per cent of all forest area altered by 1980 through tax incentives for capital investment (industrial wood production and livestock ranching); rural credits for agricultural production (mechanized agriculture, cattle ranching and silviculture); subsidized small-farmer settlement; and export subsidies.

Similarly, in Malaysia and Indonesia, government policies to encourage the switch from the export of raw logs to processed timber products have led to substantial losses in timber rents, the establishment of inefficient processing operations, and accelerated deforestation.[2] Equally problematic has been the allocation of timber concession rights, leasing agreements and the incentives for reforestation (Pearce, Barbier and Markandya, 1990; Repetto and Gillis, 1988).

These policy failures mean that the ultimate owners of the tropical forest resources – developing country governments on behalf of their people – are not extracting sufficient compensation from development activities that "use up" these resources. Instead of capturing the entire *resource rent* – the full resource value except for the cost of labour and capital employed in managing and harvesting – these governments are allowing forest resources to be used too cheaply. The result is overexploitation by individuals after quick profits. Thus policy failures leading to poor rent capture has several effects:

it means that developing countries are being insufficiently compensated for the depletion of their forest resources;

it encourages "rent-seeking" behaviour, i.e. an acceleration in the rate of deforestation as those responsible for forest-clearing and overexploitation seek to secure even larger and larger rents; and

it leads to a policy emphasis on maximizing production from forest *development* activities (timber extraction, agricultural production, mining) as a means for governments to increase their revenues.

Box 8.7 indicates government rent capture from tropical timber in five countries. By not charging sufficient stumpage fees and taxes or by selling harvesting rights too cheaply, by and large most governments have allowed the resource rents

---

Box 8.7   **Tropical Timber Rent Capture**

	(US$ million)			
	Potential Rent from Log Harvest (1)	*Actual Rent from Log Harvest (2)*	*Official Gov't Rent Capture (3)*	*3/2 (%)*	*3/1 (%)*
Indonesia (1979–82)	4954	4409	1644	37.3	33.2
Sabah (Malaysia, 1979–82)	2198	2094	1703	81.3	77.5
Philippines (1979–82)	1505	1033	171	16.5	11.4
Philippines (1987)	256	68	39	57.1	15.3
Ivory Coast	204	188	59	31.5	28.9
Ghana		80	30	38.0	

Sources: R. Repetto, "Macroeconomic Policies and Deforestation", prepared for UNU/WIDER Project *The Environment and Emerging Development Issues*, 1990; R. Repetto and M. Gillis (eds), *Public Policies and the Misuse of Forest Resources*, Cambridge University Press, Cambridge, 1988.

to flow to timber concessionaires and speculators as excess profits.

For example, in the Philippines, if the government had been able to collect its full share of actual rents, its timber revenues would have exceeded US$250 million – nearly six times the US$39 million actually collected. Instead, profits of at least US$4500 per hectare went to timber concessionaires, mill owners and timber traders (Repetto, 1990). Although the total area of production forest in the Philippines is 4.4 million ha, the total area under timber concession exceeds this at nearly 5.7 million ha – almost 90 per cent of the entire forest area. Concessions are generally awarded for twenty-five years but some for as little as five, even though the minimum realistic felling cycle is thirty years and the rotation sixty years. Almost all the large logging companies have senior politicians on their boards, and it is generally the politicians, not forestry officials, who ultimately determine concession policy and allocation (Poore *et al.*, 1989, ch. 5).

In addition, government-financed investment programmes – for road-building, colonial settlement and large-scale agricultural and mining activities – may *indirectly* be contributing to deforestation by "opening up" frontier areas that were previously inaccessible to smallholders and migrants. For example, in Brazil, the major factor determining future pressure for deforestation is the growth of small-scale agriculture, including cattle-raising, mostly in the states of Rondonia, Acre and Para. In the past, federal road-building programmes in the Brazilian Amazon have had an important influence on this pressure (see Box 8.8). As long as access to new forest lands is assured by continued road-building, these lands will always be relatively cheap for individuals to obtain. Moreover, as long as there is always additional, cheap forest land to exploit, individuals will move from areas where land is scarce to clear and burn the new land for agriculture and pasture. Frontier agriculture will therefore push deeper and deeper into the forest, until new land becomes less accessible and thus more costly to exploit.

Since 1979, around 540,000 families have been resettled in the Outer Islands from the more populated Inner Islands of

Box 8.8   Road-building and Deforestation: The Brazilian Amazon

For a long time, road-building has been thought of as an important influence on the rate of tropical deforestation. Past estimates for Brazil allege that road-building may have accounted for as much as one-quarter of deforestation. The figure is difficult to measure, as road-building's direct effects on deforestation may be overshadowed by its indirect effects via "opening up" new frontier lands for agricultural exploitation.

The table presents the changes in the densities of deforestated area, road-building and other major indicators of the expansion of the agricultural frontier for the states of the Legal Amazon over the period 1975–85.

Changes in the Densities of Deforested Area, Farm Area,
Crop Area, Squatter Area, Population, Cattle and Roads
Legal Amazon, 1975–85[1]

	Defor. Area	Farm Area	Crop Area	Squat. Area	Cattle	Roads	Pop.
Rondonia	12.7	12.6	1.45	1.48	3.0	5.86	3.3
Maranhao	10.7	11.4	0.96		6.0		6.4
Mato Grosso	8.8	19.1	2.03		4.2	5.16	1.1
Para	8.0	6.4	1.70	−0.67	1.6	1.78	1.7
Tocantins	6.2	10.1	1.21		5.0		1.2
Acre	5.0	10.6	0.18	1.18	1.4	2.70	1.0
Roraima	1.5	1.9	0.00	−5.06	0.3	1.69	0.3
Amazonas	1.2	0.1	0.05	0.61	0.1	0.15	0.5
Amapa	0.5	3.8	0.07	1.20	−0.1	5.19	0.7
Legal Amazon	5.6	7.3	0.62		1.9	2.63	1.4

Notes: 1. Units are per cent of state area for deforestation, farm, crop and squatter area; inhabitants per sq. km. for population; animal units per sq. km. for cattle; and metres per sq. km. for roads.
Source: E. Reis and S. Margulis, "Options for Slowing Amazon Jungle-Clearing", Paper presented at Conference on Economic Policy Responses for Global Warming, Rome, 5–7 September, 1990.

At state level, changes in deforestation appear to be generally related to increasing road density, which also appears to be linked to changes in the other indicators of agricultural frontier expansion. The one exception is Amapa, which has an inordinately high level of road density and the lowest level of deforestation. The relationship is, however, stronger at the municipality level.

Indonesia through official programmes. By the end of the 1980s, about one million hectares of forest land will have been converted to agricultural land for transmigration. However, the ending of official transmigration in recent years has not stopped spontaneous migration to the Outer Islands – much of it initially attracted to existing frontier settlement areas – which is probably responsible for an additional one million ha converted over the 1980s (Pearce, Barbier and Markandya, 1990, ch. 5).

There is also evidence of *non-economic* policy distortions contributing to extensive deforestation.[3] Formal property law and titling regulations often ensure that clearing of land is a pre-requisite for guaranteeing claims to frontier forest landholdings. Given the insecurity of many frontier tenure regimes, private individuals and firms often excessively clear forest lands in order to safeguard their tenuous claims to holdings and to "capture" agricultural rents. For example, a statistical analysis of defor-estation in Ecuador indicated that the extent of land-clearing for agriculture was a function not only of rural population pressure but also of tenure insecurity (Southgate, Sierra and Brown, 1989).

As the capacity of many governments to "manage" vast tracts of publicly owned tropical forests is often minimal, encroachment into forest reserves and protected lands is not controlled. At the same time, proper consideration of cus-tomary land tenure arrangements and access claims by indig-enous forest-dwellers and users is often lacking in govern-ment decisions to allocate forest land or determine titling. The failure to recognize explicitly the *adat* (customary law) rights of traditional cultivators within forest boundaries in the Outer Islands of Indonesia and the resulting absence of secure tenure give rise to an increase in shifting cultivation, and thus to deforestation. Attempts to resettle shifting cultivators into sedentary agriculture have generally not been successful; for example, between 1972 and 1982 only 10,000 families were resettled (Pearce, Barbier and Markandya, 1990, ch. 5).

Utilizing Degraded Forest Land

Land degradation is the end consequence of rapid deforestation. Too often, as converted forest land becomes degraded it is abandoned as individuals seek new and more productive forested areas to convert and exploit. Improving the incentive to stay on/restore degraded forest land by raising its productivity may be a critical component of policies for lowering the incentives to excessive deforestation. For example, if incentives to exploit new land are reduced without raising the productivity of degraded land, degradation of accessible new land will continue.

However, seemingly "obvious" technical solutions may not be the answer. For example, it is often argued that the development of plantations on degraded lands is the solution to prevent unnecessary harvesting of virgin forest – the annual increment may be more than ten times as great per hectare. None the less, it has also been proved financially attractive to establish plantations by clearing new forest rather than by planting previously cleared land: the soils are more fertile and there are fewer problems of land tenure (Poore *et al.*, 1989, ch. 10). The fact that there is a potential role for forest plantation on degraded land does not preclude other land-use options from being more beneficial. Again, appropriate cost-benefit analysis of alternative land-use options is necessary.

Similarly, devising new technical packages and alternative cropping systems are necessary but not sufficient to solve the degraded land problem (see Box 8.9). It is necessary to develop markets for the products these systems will produce and to ensure that value-added is captured by local communities.

Suitable marketing systems must also be evaluated, and just as in the case of forested lands, cost-benefit analysis of alternative land-use options for the degraded lands must also be devised. In certain cases, it may even be sensible to allow some abandoned forest land to regenerate naturally. Finally, it is also important to correct market and policy distortions which work against the successful exploitation of degraded

Box 8.9 **Alternatives to Slash-and-burn Agriculture**

Shifting cultivation – slash-and-burn – systems are not generally sustainable except at low population densities. A sustainable alternative is needed which offers a reasonable return to inputs and standard of living for small-scale farmers. However, shifting cultivation is attractive to farmers under conditions where land is abundant relative to labour and capital. Fertilizers and other cash inputs are generally not used because of their high prices.

For example, in the "northern colonization zone" above Santa Cruz, Bolivia, a colonist normally receives a plot of 30 to 50 ha of forest land from which all valuable timber has already been removed by concessionaires. Under this system, the average farmer cultivates about two hectares of annual crops, virtually all rice, during the wet season. Farmers also diversify into perennial crops and livestock production, but rice is seen to be the paramount output of the system. The following table shows the average input requirements for the system:

Average Inputs for Rice Shifting Cultivation

Man days/ha

Forest Felling and Land Preparation	20–40
Sowing	3
Weeding	20
Spraying	2
Harvesting	25
Threshing and Post-Harvest	4

Other Inputs/ha

Seeds	20 kg
Herbicide	8 litres

Source: J. Wilkins, "The Search for a Viable Alternative to Slash and Burn Agriculture in the Lowland Plains of Bolivia", *Expl Agric.*, Vol. 27, 1991, forthcoming.

Average rice yields from this system are about 1850 kg per ha. The average family of six consumes about 385 kg of rice per year. Thus only 0.33 ha of rice is required for subsistence, the rest of the crop being sold. However, the returns to selling rice normally provide only less than 25% of the family's required income.

Several improvements and alternatives to the system are being developed, with the aim of providing more sustainable and better livelihoods:

- using leguminous forage species instead of a forest fallow in rotation with annual crops;
- continuous cultivation of annual crops with alleys of leguminous shrubs (*alley cropping*);
- growing tree crops on 0.5 ha (cocoa, coffee, citrus and banana, and possibly macadamia, cashew, peach palm and coconuts);
- dual-purpose milk/beef silvo-pastoral systems, initially with sheep, then possibly cattle.

Although these more intensive alternatives are technically feasible, they have economic consequences for farmers that must be resolved, such as the high risks of switching from more to less familiar cropping systems and outputs, possible difficulties with marketing, post-harvest handling, credit and input availability, high input requirements, longer "waiting costs" before returns are realized and, not least, fluctuations in input and output prices.

lands. For example, brazil nuts are subject to an export tax that has encouraged illicit sales to Bolivia, with the result that value-added is lost to Brazil and an important crop for degraded lands is underexploited.

Conclusion

Excessive tropical deforestation is a matter of concern for both tropical forest countries and the international community. In this chapter we have stressed the importance of proper valuation of forest resources, cost-benefit analysis of land-use options for both forested and degraded lands, and correcting market and policy distortions that both work against the incentives for restoring or improving degraded lands and increase the financial attractiveness of overexploiting and converting tropical forests.

However, tropical forests may have some important economic values that are internationally significant. In particular, their functions as "stores" of carbon and biological diversity may have a global value. As argued in this chapter, as other nations benefit from these global values, they should be willing to pay tropical forest countries for conserving the forests. Not only is it important to begin estimating these values in monetary terms, it is also essential to begin discussing appropriate international transfer mechanisms and agreements through which these values can be translated into financial resource flows that can benefit tropical forest countries directly. Some options currently being discussed include:

> compensatory financing under the forthcoming international climate convention;
> establishment of a biodiversity fund;
> debt-for-nature swaps; and
> the World Bank Global Environmental Facility.

In addition, the emergence of the International Tropical Timber Organization (ITTO), which is essentially a commodity organization bringing together the major tropical timber consumers, traders and producers as a basis for formulating a policy consensus on the trade, is an important step in encouraging more effective global efforts to bring tropical forests under sustained management. At the same time, the ITTO may be effective in discouraging well-meaning but unhelpful policy developments concerning the trade, such as a ban on tropical timber imports proposed by some consumer nations.[4]

Notes

1. For recent comparative reviews of how public policies affect deforestation, see Pearce, Barbier and Markandya (1990); Repetto (1990) and Repetto and Gillis (1988).
2. The term *rent* here refers to *economic rent*; i.e. the difference between the full market value of the timber and the costs of labour and capital employed in managing and harvesting it. Unless governments, who are generally the proprietors of forest resources, extract the rent through taxation and concession policies, it will instead accrue to the harvesters of the resource as excess profits.
3. For a review, see Binswanger (1989); Mahar (1989) and Pearce, Barbier and Markandya (1990), chs 5 and 9.
4. The use of bans on highly valued resource commodities that also have very widely dispersed, and fluid, trading routes has not been very successful. In general, a controlled and regulated trade linked to the sustainable management practices may be more effective. In this regard, the lessons from the economic analysis of the trade in elephant ivory might be instructive for the timber trade (see Barbier *et al.*, 1990).

References

Barbier, E.B., J.C. Burgess, T.S. Swanson, and D.W. Pearce (1990), *Elephants, Economics and Ivory*, London: Earthscan.

Binswanger, H. (1989), *Brazilian Policies that Encourage Deforestation in the Amazon*, Environment Department Working Paper No. 16, Washington, DC: World Bank.

Mahar, D. (1989), *Government Policies and Deforestation in Brazil's Amazon Region*, Washington, DC: World Bank.

Pearce, D.W. (1990), *An Economic Approach to Saving the Tropical Forests*, LEEC Paper 90-05, London: London Environmental Economics Centre.

Pearce, D.W., E.B. Barbier, and A. Markandya (1990), *Sustainable Development: Economics and Environment in the Third World*, London: Edward Elgar.

Poore, D., F. Burgess, J. Palmer, S. Reitbergen, and T. Synott (1989), *No Timber Without Trees: Sustainability in the Tropical Forest*, London: Earthscan.

Repetto, R. (1990). "Macroeconomic Policies and Deforestation", paper prepared for UNU/WIDER Project *The Environment and Emerging Development Issues*, Helsinki.

Repetto, R. and M. Gillis (1988), *Public Policies and the Misuse of Forest Resources*, Cambridge: Cambridge University Press.

Repetto, R., M. Wells, C. Beer, and F. Rossini (1987), *Natural Resource Accounting for Indonesia*, Washington, DC: World Resources Institute.

Schmidt, R.C. (1989), *Current Tropical Moist Forest Management Activities in Brazil*, report prepared for the government of Brazil, Rome: FAO.

Southgate, D., R. Sierra, and L. Brown (1989), *The Causes of Tropical Deforestation in Ecuador: A Statistical Analysis*, LEEC Paper 89-09, London: London Environmental Economics Centre.

9

Environmentally Sensitive Aid

R. Kerry Turner

Introduction

The focus of this chapter is the environmental degradation now being suffered by the poorer nations of the South and the positive role that donor assistance (aid) can play in the alleviation of the problem. The environmental damage (loss of tropical forests, wetlands, desertification, etc.) that has taken place and is still occurring in developing countries is of course not merely a national concern but has potentially significant international and even global ramifications. Thus the environmental degradation in any one country can impact on the well-being of another country. Tropical deforestation in a developing country may be justified domestically because the benefits of deforestation are judged to outweigh the costs borne nationally.[1] A developed country secures little or no benefit from that same deforestation process, but may well suffer costs in the form of climate impacts, concern over loss of biological diversity, and so on. Not surprisingly, poorer nations seeking the benefits of rapid industrialization may well resent international expressions of concern about resource degradation.

What is important in this simplistic international environmental degradation example is that transfer payments ("aid flows") have a positive role to play. Official development assistance exceeds $40 billion a year. In the case of forestry, perhaps the developed country should "pay" the developing country not to deforest.[2] If it is accepted that an environmental interdependency does exist between North and South, then there are probably opportunities for mutual gain by bargaining. Both North and South, it can be argued, have a common interest in environmental conservation and preservation.

These interdependency arguments should not, however, be overemphasized. They may not on their own be enough to convince national policy-makers of the need for new multi-lateral programmes of action. Mutual interests (achieved via exchange) and common interests (achieved via co-operation) of a general nature are all too easily dominated by national interests. The effect of official foreign aid is of course only a small part of the total impact of the developed countries on the environment and peoples of the developing world. Aid has to be seen in the context of these wider international economic and political relationships. Critics of Western aid programmes and the international economic relationships that underpin them have long argued that the dominant feature of these relation-ships is expropriation. According to this critical viewpoint, wealth has flowed and still flows from the developing world to Europe, the USA, Japan, and a few other countries. It is this expropriation process that lies at the core of the environmental destruction and continued poverty in developing countries. A general feature of aid, it is claimed, is that it is useful to the firms and exporters of the developed countries providing it. Whether or not the aid is tied to particular projects, most of it is "tied" to producers of goods and services in the donor countries.

Most multilateral aid-givers also incorporate "conditionality" constraints on their aid, in order to secure policy changes by the recipient governments. The conditions (structural adjustment programmes) cover not only the type of project to be supported but general macroeconomic policy, for example, removal of food subsidies and devaluation of the currency.[3]

This radical critique of the international political economy may or may not be totally convincing, but what is less con-tentious is that during the 1970s and for most of the 1980s confidence in and support for international institutions di-minished. It is only very recently that global/international environmental problems seem to have renewed interest in multilateral co-operation (e.g. the Montreal Protocol on CFCS and the North Sea waste-dumping Protocol). Nevertheless, economic growth/development issues are intimately tied up with environmental issues, and both the magnitude and extensiveness of the environmental degradation process appear to be increasing.

Conventional Aid Flows and the Environment

Official foreign aid (with its emphasis on large projects, dams, power stations, infrastructure, etc.) has at times contributed to the destruction of forests and other environmental resources. It has also persistently failed to improve the general condition of the poorest sectors of the population in developing countries. This was despite the fact that during the 1970s a new "poverty-focus" for aid (made operational by selection of "appropriate" projects) was adopted; and during the second half of the 1980s multilateral agencies began to address the issue of the environmental consequences of their aid-giving. One multilateral, the World Bank, has recently begun to screen its project lending to determine the environmental component in its agricultural, forestry and rural development projects. It was noted that project design rarely included environmental considerations, and longer-term evaluations after project implementation suggested a fairly high incidence of environmental damage.

The surveys also found that donor guidance to aid-recipient countries had traditionally been limited; inadequate attention was paid to institutional weaknesses, land tenure problems and the broader package of measures needed to integrate natural resource concerns into investments. Often, major changes within a country were ignored, for example, the impact of massive population migration in Brazil and Indonesia on the resource base. Lending was often "opportunistic", based on initiatives within, say, a government department rather than on an integrated programme approach. The inclusion of environmental assessments in project evaluation also made little difference to the procedures for selecting and designing projects.[4] That is to say, simply insisting on environmental assessments had little effect on the criteria actually used in selecting projects.

As aid donors have increasingly made use of structural and sectoral adjustment, it is important to review what effect this policy may have had on environmental quality. Early experience with project lending showed that projects could fail because of distortions in the developing-country economy – excessive protection, exchange rate control, subsidies, etc. This, together with debt-servicing problems, seems to be the rationale for adjustment lending. But have structural adjustment loans themselves caused environmental degradation?

The evidence, such as it is, is mixed. There are widely quoted examples of the policy encouraging export-orientated crop production through price and credit incentives. It is then assumed either that the export crops are themselves environmentally destructive, or that their encouragement forces subsistence farming on to ecologically fragile marginal land. Adjustment policies include a wide range of instruments – price manipulation (up and down); agricultural export tax adjustments; currency devaluations; agricultural and energy subsidy reductions; trade liberalization and public expenditure reductions. Generalizations are difficult to support conclusively, but it is not true that adjustment policy inevitably degrades the environment. It depends on the type of adjustment policy and the actual sector of the economy that is being affected. In cases where short-to-medium-term macroeconomic adjustments have been imposed, there is a real danger that poverty levels would have increased. This then has serious implications for the environment, given the links between poverty and the environment.

International Economic Relations: The Debt Crisis

The prolonged recession in the international economy has meant that all economies, developed and developing, have had to undergo structural readjustments, but the poorest economies have had to face a disproportionate adjustment problem. The combination of slow growth in world trade, rising debt-service obligations and a lack of new inward financial flows has resulted in severe economic crises. Half of all developing countries have experienced a fall in *per capita* GDP over the period 1982 to 1985; as a group, developing economies saw their GDP *per capita* fall by 10 per cent during the 1980s. In 1980 the developing countries accounted for 28 per cent of the dollar value of world exports, but by 1986 their share had fallen to 19 per cent.

The heaviest burden in international economic adjustment has had to be carried by those groups least able to respond effectively to the external pressures, the world's poorest people. Two main consequences have arisen:

(i) a considerable increase in human distress;
(ii) overexploitation of land and natural resources by the poor in order to try to ensure survival in the short term, at the inevitable expense of long-run sustainability.

By the end of the 1980s, aid donor policies requiring structural adjustments to facilitate continued debt-servicing, together with relative price declines for many developing-country export commodities, have meant that production, investment, imports and income per head had all declined in many developing economies.

The crisis has been particularly severe in Africa. Debt service rose in Sub-Saharan Africa as a whole from 15 per cent of export earnings in 1980 to 31 per cent in 1986. This combination of events has led to a situation where net resource transfers (i.e. net loan transfers, grants and net direct investments minus net direct investment income) to the area fell from an estimated $10 billion per annum in 1982 to only $1 billion in 1985. More long-term financial assistance is urgently required for these African countries, but a larger proportion of total development assistance should go to investments needed to enhance the environment and the productivity of the resource sectors. Experience has shown that the most effective projects in this context are small-scale projects, often designed to rehabilitate existing systems and requiring the involvement of community organizations. Properly costed (by extended CBA and environmental impact assessment [EIA]), such schemes can be shown to be both economically viable and environmentally sustainable.

A Poverty-focus for Aid

As we have seen, concern with the effects of aid on the environment is a relatively recent phenomenon. It has parallels with a longer-standing concern about its effects on poverty, and the two areas overlap. Pragmatic arguments based on self-interest may be used to reinforce the ethical arguments in favour of aid designed to reduce inequalities in current generations of humans as well as protecting the welfare of unrepresented future generations. Poverty is a major cause and effect of global environmental problems. Poverty, which denies people the means to act in their own long-term interest, creates environmental stress, leading to resource degradation and growing population pressures. This environmental stress could reach a stage at which global welfare is threatened, regardless of whether one lives in a developing or developed economy.

The pressure of poverty must be seen in an international context. Unacceptably large differences exist in *per capita* income levels, which ranged from $190 in low-income countries (excluding India and China) to $11,430 in industrial market economies in 1984.

Opinions differ over the effect of structural and sector adjustment programmes on the poor in developing countries. The official aim of adjustment lending is to secure desirable "adjustments" in the borrowing economy and to mitigate the effects of these adjustments, particularly in the balance of payments. Some measurements in the adjustment programmes may have benefited the poor – increases in food prices and other agricultural products, through devaluation and other mechanisms, could have benefited small farmers. Much depends, however, on the exact type of crop that is affected, and on whether the farmers concerned produce a surplus for the market at all. Higher food prices do not benefit the landless, the urban poor or farmers (usually a majority of the poor) who have no surplus to sell. On the other hand, these groups may have benefited from other adjustment policies which have lowered the price of some food crops such as rice, maize and sorghum.

It is also not necessarily true that aid policy directed at alleviating environmental degradation will always be complementary to the poverty-alleviation objective. A policy to protect forests, for example, can mean keeping poor people out of them. Nevertheless, since the late 1980s the environmental sensitivity and poverty-alleviation focuses for aid have been converging. They have combined to put more pressure on the aid agencies to monitor and evaluate the effects of their schemes.

Sustainability and the Economic Calculus

The moral case for aid requires a wider focus, and that focus is on bringing environmental resources into the economic calculus. Economic analysis and economic factors can play a positive role in the attainment of a more socially desirable and sustainable future. While monetary value is inadequate as the sole criterion for decisions, the benefit-cost approach and rationale is generally applicable. This approach involves systematically accounting for all the consequences (positive and negative) that stem from alternative projects, policies or programmes. If it can be demonstrated (and in many development/environment policy and project contexts this is so) that the present costs of new policies and programmes undertaken now is small relative to the subsequent costs or the long-run damage costs that will be incurred if no action is taken, then these actions are both economically viable and environmentally attractive.

Bilateral and multilateral development agencies need, however, to improve their assessments of projects which could have damaging impacts on critical ecosystems and species. Project finances should include provisions for compensatory set-aside schemes where critical environmental assets are threatened. Efforts should be made at governmental level to begin a process of negotiation leading to a "Species Convention". This would help to fund the network of "protected" natural areas, and to counteract common property overexploitation tendencies. The sustainable development strategy implies a "managerial" approach to the whole set of natural, human, financial and physical assets, so that over the long term the basic needs of all humans are met and opportunities for increased well-being are widened considerably.

Decision criteria for judging the social desirability of policies and projects would include economic efficiency (not as a meta-criterion) alongside equity and other considerations. Agencies such as the IMF and the World Bank, among others, should be encouraged to adopt extended cost-benefit analysis and environmental impact analysis techniques as routine elements in their project appraisal processes.

The use of these multicriteria methods would counterbalance the influence of the overly restrictive conventional (i.e. economic-efficiency-based) cost-benefit analysis technique, which has tended to neglect broader social and environmental project impacts. Thus, for example, water resource projects should be assessed in terms of their contribution to the efficiency of resource usage in a system-wide context. Impacts on upland watersheds, on water-borne diseases, on soil structures and on the socioeconomic structure of local communities, for example, all need to be encompassed within the planning/assessment process.

Economic and environmental problems cannot be completely divorced from social and political problems. Thus sustainability must encompass social objectives – for example improving the status of women in developing-country societies; provision of better protection for vulnerable groups, especially children; and the promotion of local participation in decision-making.

The general principles of sustainability must be tailored and refined to fit local circumstances. Thus, for example, the Asian "Green Revolution" model is totally inappropriate for African agriculture. The Asian model had as its cornerstone improved crop varieties, which in turn were dependent on fertilizer inputs, controlled water supplies, good soil and good management. In Africa, labour is scarce, irrigation is not widespread, soils are often poor and rainfall is unreliable. Faced with an extremely sensitive environment, the African smallholder operates in a distinctive way. He is often desperately poor and therefore operates on short time horizons in a very risk-averse fashion. Any strategy aimed at mitigating rural poverty, malnutrition and environmental destruction in Africa must contain the following elements: a focus on smallholders, input packages and techniques (especially soil conservation techniques) based on careful on-farm research; community participation; credit facilities requiring repayment only after crop sales; high average returns on investment; agricultural price rises.[5]

Key Intervention Points for Sustainable Development

It is possible to construct a simple matrix to facilitate better understanding of at what level and how aid donors could encourage intervention in the socioeconomic and supporting ecosystems of developing countries, in order to promote more sustainable development. Figure 9.1 summarizes the main points:

(a) The household/community level is critically important and offers considerable scope for intervention channelled through non-governmental organizations (NGOs). The provision of credit for small farmers is a high priority need here.
(b) Aid packages channelled through technology/extension services, as well as information and competence-building initiatives, are important if natural resource degradation is to be alleviated. Further, these initiatives have to be disseminated across all levels, from community through to the region.
(c) Aid donors should be encouraged to specialize in specific ecozone types (e.g. arid zones, etc.) in order to improve the overall cost-effectiveness of aid-giving.
(d) Once donors begin to concentrate their attention on given ecological zone types then specific technical, informational and other expertise can be accumulated and will be tailored to the specific problems of the targeted zone. A more accurate and comprehensive understanding of zone-specific environmental effects can then be built up and aid targeted in a more rational manner.

(e) The debt burden (in terms of an insolvency problem) that most of the poorer countries have built up has set in motion a natural resource degradation process because of the extension of cash cropping, often on to marginal land. Where there are strong links between debt-service burden and increasing environmental damage, there is a strong argument in favour of interest rate reductions or debt cancellation.

Box 9.1   **Intervention Points for Sustainable Development**

Areas of Concern	DEVELOPMENT PROGRAMMES	INFORMATION+ TECHNOLOGY+ COMPETENCE	MACRO POLICIES
HOUSEHOLD/ COMMUNITY	People sensitive, localised, critical area for NGOs	This is the critical area —for— environmentally sensitive aid	
ECO-ZONES			
COUNTRY	Present focus of aid		Area of conditionality; politically sensitive
REGION	potentially important for small countries		
INTERNATIONAL COMMUNITY		Traditional area of multi-lateral effort must be made environmentally sensitive	

Source: R. Kerry Turner, "Economics and Environmentally Sensitive Aid", *International Journal of Environmental Studies*, 35, 39–50, 1989.

By the end of the 1980s "environmental sensitivity" thinking had penetrated fairly deeply into aid-giving circles. The World Bank procedures for appraising projects, for example, had become much stricter with reference to environmental impacts.[6] More than a third of projects approved in fiscal year 1989 contained significant environmental components. New directives on environmental assessment in projects are under formulation, and the aim is to extend this to sector work.

There is still, however, much scope for further initiatives in the "environmental sensitivity" context. The next section summarizes some of the options that are available.

Options for International Conservation Financing

One of the more radical suggestions made in order to "reform" the aid-giving process involves the direct transfer of lump-sum payments from donors for "non-development", free of any conditionality. So far no such transfers have occurred.

Another option involves the transfer of compensatory resources to avoid environmental damage by developing some other environmentally less destructive route. This transfer may take the form of technical assistance and loans that are specific to environmentally benign projects. Some progress has been made in this context by the World Bank and other agencies.

A third option involves transfers which reduce some obligation by developing countries to developed countries in return for reduced environmental destruction and sustainable management of natural resources. Structural adjustment loans could include some form of environmental "conditionality", or so-called "debt-for-nature" swaps could be arranged. There are a growing number of examples of these types of transfer.

One recent study has suggested four ways of developing "conservation financing":[7]

(i) A Global Environmental Facility, aimed at funding a range of conservation projects not currently funded by existing agencies. Donor countries have been (in 1990) discussing a proposal for a facility to finance programmes in developing countries that would address global environmental objectives – ozone layer protection, greenhouse gas emissions reductions, international water resource protection and biodiversity protection. A multilateral fund to assist developing countries to substitute for chlorofluorocarbons has already been agreed, with additional funding of $160 billion.

(ii) "Ecovests", the main function of which would be the demonstration of the private profitability of some environmentally benign investments such as wildlife utilization and "ecotourism".

(iii) "Debt-for-nature" swaps. The idea of such a swap is that a conservation group, for example, could buy some second-hand international debt of a developing country.[8] It then agrees to "swap" the debt for an agreement relating the conservation in the indebted country. The indebted country reduces its debt; the conservationists secure increased conservation.[9]

(iv) A Global Environmental Trust Fund: this would be established by securing a levy or tax on a global pollutant such as carbon dioxide. The proceeds of the levy would then be "recycled" to countries who face difficulties in reducing carbon emissions, for example by funding energy conservation and afforestation.

A number of debt-for-nature swaps have taken place: a US environmental organization bought up Bolivian debt and swapped it for an agreement with the Bolivian government to establish and legally protect three conservation zones (2.7 million acres) adjacent to the Beni Biosphere Reserve, which had been established in 1982, and to enhance the legal protection of the reserve itself. Under the agreement half the forest was protected for scientific investigation and indigenous rights, but half was scheduled for sustainable logging. This latter provision has been much criticized.

Other examples of debt-for-nature swap agreements include an agreement between the government of Costa Rica and the World Wide Fund for Nature and other agencies in 1987–8, resulting in the establishment of a Natural Resources Conservation Fund in Costa Rica. Further swap agreements with the Dutch and Swedish governments have followed. The World Wide Fund for Nature has also completed swap deals with Ecuador, the Philippines, Madagascar and Zambia.

A number of criticisms have been levelled at these swap arrangements:

(a) They have an insignificant effect on developing-country indebtedness. The counter-argument here would be that their primary purpose was nature conservation, not debt reduction *per se*.

(b) Loss of national sovereignty: developing-country governments and people living in and around the conservation zones lose control over an important part of their natural assets in return for a very small dilution of debt.

(c) They are inflationary. This is questionable, since the amounts in question are small and the conversion process in two cases was to bonds, not cash.

(d) Host governments will renege on the management agreement.

(e) Domestic poor people may be displaced by conservation designation.

Overall, the real contribution of debt-to-nature swaps is probably that they have at least raised awareness in developing countries that sustainable development is a priority issue.

Notes

1. At the early stages of development the perceived value of natural environments frequently appears to be low. Priority is given to industrialization and development programmes which often damage the environment. In contrast, environmental values and concerns in richer developed countries are relatively high and currently near the top of political agendas.

2. Application of the "polluter pays" principle suggests that the polluter (the developing country) should pay the sufferer (the

developed country) for the damage caused. But since the forests belong to the developing country, property rights are vested in that country and this suggests that the sufferer should pay the polluter not to deforest. Where the damage is reciprocal, or a mix of reciprocal and unidirectional externality, the principles are less easy to derive. However, the basic observation is that there are opportunities for mutual gain by bargaining.

3. See T. Hayter, *Exploited Earth: Britain's Aid and the Environment*, Earthscan, London, 1989. Hayter allows only one caveat in this general critique of aid-giving: that there were some limited exceptions to varying degrees and in different periods – for example aid from Scandinavia, especially Sweden, and from the Netherlands, especially in the 1970s.

4. The World Bank's procedures were revised in 1971 to include reference to environmental impacts. In 1984 a statement on the environmental consequences of projects became mandatory in staff appraisal reports.

5. See P. Harrison, *The Greening of Africa*, Paladin, London, 1987.

6. See J. Warford and Z. Partow, *World Bank Support for the Environment: A Progress Report*, World Bank/IMF Development Committee Paper No.22, Washington, DC, September 1989.

7. World Resources Institute, *Natural Endowments: Financing Resource Conservation for Development*, World Resources Institute, Washington, DC, September 1989.

8. Debt/equity swaps evolved as a mechanism for reducing developing-country debts that built up during the 1980s. (There was some $1300 billion of outstanding international debt related to developing countries at the end of 1987.) Under this system some of the commercial banks' debt certificates can be bought at large discounts on the secondary market. It is then possible, with the agreement of the World Bank/IMF and relevant governments, to use the certificates to "buy up" selected assets in the debtor country. Debt-for-nature swaps follow the same principle.

9. See S. Hansen, "Debt for Nature Swaps – Overview and Discussion of Key Issues, *Ecological Economics*, 1, 1989, pp. 77–93.

10

Conserving Biological Diversity

Tim Swanson

Maintenance versus Preservation

The global loss of biological diversity, or "biodiversity", is currently one of the major problems facing the world. It was recognized as such in the publication of the *World Conservation Strategy* in 1980. In the interim period, several movements have developed for the purpose of preserving the remaining areas of significant biological diversity, i.e. natural habitat. These include the establishment of national parks and wilderness areas, the arrangement of "debt-for-nature" swaps, and even a proposed international convention for the development of an international fund for the conservation of biological diversity.

These measures have attained a certain amount of success. For example, almost 5 per cent of remaining tropical forest has received some form of legal protection. On the other hand, they can only have a very limited amount of success, because they do not address the forces which generate the losses in biological diversity. For this reason, the rate at which unprotected natural habitats are being lost remains largely undiminished.

Preservation has been an approach to saving natural habitat which has been focused on the "tip of the iceberg". It is necessary to broaden this approach in a way that will address the importance of maintaining the 95 per cent of natural habitat which is currently unprotected. In addition, the strategy of preservation is subject to concerns about its long-term viability. This is because a promise to protect a designated area is much more readily kept while other areas are available for development. At current rates of exploitation, the entire remaining unprotected natural habitat will be subject to some development within the next century. Preservation areas will come under increasing pressure as this buffer stock is eroded.

Finally, the idea of preservation has been promoted in a way which renders it antithetical to development. The maintenance of natural habitat has been viewed as wholly inconsistent with the development process. In part, this is necessarily true, but it is not always so. It is also possible to develop natural habitat areas in ways which allow local communities to acquire significant uses of those resources, while also maintaining the biological diversity of the habitat. This is the core of the idea of maintaining natural habitats by harnessing the forces for development, rather than battling against them. Constructive utilization of the resources in natural habitats can act to provide the incentive to keep them. This is the means by which the 95 per cent of remaining natural habitat which is unprotected might yet be maintained.

The Meaning of Biodiversity

Biological diversity, in the biologist's sense of the word, is the natural stock of genetic material within an ecosystem. This stock may be determined by the actual number of genes existing within the system. The number of genes ranges between organisms from about 1000 in bacteria to 10,000 in some fungi, and to around 100,000 for a typical mammal. The greatest number of genes actually belong to the flowering plants, whose genes often number in excess of 400,000 or more. Genes are important because they determine the particular characteristics of a given organism and encode the information which determines the specific capabilities of that organism. The greater the variety of genetic material, the greater the variety of organisms which exist or will exist in the near future.

The ecologist's idea of biological diversity is defined in terms of the ecosystem. Any given ecosystem provides a natural flow of services, in particular the flow of Net Primary (or Photosynthetic) Product (NPP); this concept represents the ecosystem's capacity to capture and utilize the energy provided by the sun. For example, inorganic matter, such as asphalt, has no capacity to utilize the power of the sun to generate new biomass; however, plants can capture the sun's energy in the form of new leafy matter, or in reproduction. From the ecologist's perspective, it is not only the absolute amount of genetic material which exists that matters, but also the relative quantities of particular organisms. Substantial alterations in the relative proportions of organisms within a given ecosystem can result in a substantial fall in NPP. For example, the removal of a large number of a particular species of tree from a hillside may make little difference to the amount of existing genetic material (so long as at least one of that species remains), but it might place the entire ecosystem in danger. This might happen if the removal of a high proportion of the trees resulted in an increased possibility of flooding, and hence in a loss of a substantial portion of ecosystem services.

The usual unit of analysis in studies of biodiversity is the number of existing species. The number of described species is around 1.4 million; however, the number of species which have not yet been catalogued far exceeds that. Best estimates place the total number of species somewhere between 5 and 10 million.

The vast majority of these species are insects, and other smaller organisms. Among the more well-studied categories, vertebrates and flowering plants, the numbers are much lower and more certain. For example, it is known that there are about 43,853 vertebrates currently in existence, of which only 4000 are mammals, 9000 are birds, 6300 are reptiles and 4184 are amphibians. By way of contrast, it is known that there are at least 50,000 different species of mollusc (Wilson, 1986).

By reason of forces largely unknown to us, the amount of natural variety is mostly constant across natural habitats which are approximately equal in size, make-up and climate. Also, there is a clear relationship between the area of the natural habitat and the variety of species which it contains. Studies of "islands" of natural habitat, whether situated in oceans or in civilization, indicate that the number of species doubles with a tenfold increase in the area of the island. Conversely, a reduction in the size of the natural habitat by 90 per cent will result in a halving of the number of species which it will contain (Wilson, 1986).

These relationships have been obtained by comparing the number of species on similar islands of differing sizes. If the larger island were instead compared with not one, but rather many islands whose areas were in combination less than the larger island, this would be more analogous to the process of reduction and fragmentation of natural habitats which is at present occurring. This fragmentation will itself contribute to some extinctions.

Of course, extinction is itself a natural process. The studies show that the natural longevity of many species lies in the range of one to ten million years. It is not any specific stock of species which is necessary to maintain biological diversity, but rather the general stock; the actual constituency of that stock has always varied across time.

The problem of biological diversity arises when the rate of extinction of species far exceeds the rate of creation. In these eras of mass extinctions, there is a potential threat to the entire global biology. In the distant past, so-called "deep time", there have been a number of such mass extinctions. There are at least five occasions indicated in the fossil record during which over 50 per cent of the then-existing animal species were rendered extinct (Raup, 1986).

Even averaging in these periods of mass extinctions, the natural rate of extinction over deep time appears to have been in the neighbourhood of 9 per cent per million years, or approximately .000009 per cent per year (Raup, 1988). That is to say, the current stock of biological diversity is the result of several billion years of mostly low-frequency mutation and extinction, which has given us a legacy which cannot be re-created in any shorter length of time. In this respect biological diversity is one of the stocks of "ancient capital", along with the fossil fuels, rich soils and ancient groundwater, which cannot be replaced once destroyed. It is an "exhaustible resource", in the phraseology of economics, which is in many cases being exhausted without ever being utilized. It is fundamental that the value of this resource be taken into account in determining its rate of utilization. This is the basic nature of the economic problem of biodiversity.

The Current Episode of Mass Extinctions – The Source of the Problem

It is estimated that about half of the world's species are contained in the remaining tropical forests, and much of the attention on the current rates of extinction is therefore focused on these regions. The so-called "megadiversity states" identified by the World Wide Fund for Nature are: Mexico, Colombia, Brazil, Zaïre, Madagascar and Indonesia – for example, four of these states alone contain approximately 75 per cent of all primate species. In sum, it is estimated that 50 to 80 per cent of the world's biological diversity is to be found in six to twelve tropical countries, including those mentioned above (Mitter-meier, 1986).

The estimates of projected species loss in the tropics over the next few decades approaches the magnitude of the previous mass extinctions. A range of estimates has been arrived at which project a total species loss of between 20 and 50 per cent. A fairly conservative estimate would seem to be that the current rate of extinction in tropical areas is about 1000 to 10,000 times the natural rate of extinction (Wilson, 1986).

These extinctions are resulting primarily from the loss of the natural habitat upon which these species depend. It was noted above that studies have demonstrated a correspondence

---

Box 10.1 **Estimates of the Current Rates of Species Extinction**

Estimate of Loss	*Basis*	*Source*
33–55% of species by 2000	forest area loss	Lovejoy (1980)
50% of species by 2000	forest area loss	Ehrlich and Ehrlich (1981)
25–30% of species by 2000	unknown	Myers (1983)
33% of species in 21st century	forest area loss	Simberloff (1986)
20–25% of species by 2025	present trends	Norton (1986)

between the loss of habitat and the extinction of a predictable proportion of species in that habitat. In fact, it has been found that the extinction of species from such losses will usually occur relatively soon after habitat modification.

For example, the Barro Colorado Island was first created by the rise of Gatun Lake during the construction of the Panama Canal; before that, it had been part of a much larger area of natural habitat. Studies by biologists surveying the island predicted that the loss of natural habitat area would ultimately result in a loss of about 15 per cent of its species; in fact, the number of bird species which had been extinguished on that island within fifty years of its creation was already equal to 12 per cent of the initial stock. Thus, the phenomenon of extinction linked to natural habitat losses can be a relatively certain, and short term, phenomenon (Terborgh, 1974).

Most of the estimates of current extinction rates flow from the use of these observed relationships between loss of natural habitat and loss of species. It currently happens that human populations are expanding and natural habitats declining, most rapidly in the zones of most diversity. The resulting rate of deforestation in the tropical zones has been estimated at between 10 and 20 million hectares per year – that is, an area approximately the size of California is lost every two years (OTA 1984). Given our current understanding of the relationship between natural habitat and species diversity, it is possible to predict the dire consequences of these losses of natural habitat for global biodiversity.

Natural habitat is declining in the face of ever-increasing human pressure for a greater share of the earth's product. As described above, the ecologist's notion of ecosystem services is Net Primary Product (NPP): the product of biological material making use of the sun's energy. Although the human species is only one amongst millions, it currently sequesters to its own purposes over 40 per cent of the earth's terrestrial product.

The problem of biodiversity lies not in the proportion of the earth's product which humans use, but rather in the proportion of the earth's product which humans deny to other species. That is, we use directly only 10 per cent of the resources which we

Box 10.2 **Human Appropriation of the Earth's Biological Product**

Net Photosynthetic Product (NPP) is the sum total of an ecosystem's flow of services in a given period of time. Although the human species is only one of about 5 to 10 million species, it prevents other species from making use of about 40 per cent of terrestrial NPP. Of this amount, humans use only about 4 per cent directly. Their production methods remove from the use of other species another 36 per cent, which is not directly consumed by humans. Of this, about 26 per cent represents indirect use – e.g. unused produce returned to the earth – while another 10 per cent represents pure waste, e.g. asphalted soil.

Use	Share of NPP
Direct Use	4%
Indirect Use	26%
Losses	10%
Total	40%

Source: P. Vitousek, P. Ehrlich, A. Ehrlich and P. Matson (1986), "Human Appropriation of the Products of Photosynthesis", *Bioscience*, vol. 36, no. 6, pp. 368–73.

reserve to ourselves; the other resources we deny to other species because of the manner in which we take our 4 per cent of NPP.

The above figures indicate that we reduce NPP a full 10 per cent, more than twice what we consume, in terms of pure wastage. This results most dramatically when good soil is paved under for a road, but also occurs when a natural forest or pasture is ploughed under to produce a common commodity such as corn. The total biomass of the ecosystem is often reduced by virtue of the replacement of a vast quantity of different species with a single one. This is because species are expert at finding an available niche in which to prosper. The natural stock of biological diversity has resulted largely from this natural process of niche identification. The replacement of this natural diversity with a single species will very often leave a large number of such niches unfilled, thus resulting in a net loss in ecosystem product.

The far more significant figure is the amount of ecosystem services which we indirectly use; this constitutes a full 26 per cent of total NPP. These uses include the parts of the plants we grow which are not consumed by us, and thus return to the earth unused by a higher organism. It also includes the amount of biological matter which is cleared and burned in the agricultural process. All this material could be used by higher species before its return to the earth, but this use is denied to them by humans in the process of creating the 4 per cent of NPP which is ultimately used.

It is not really a problem that the human species directly consumes 4 per cent of NPP; given the size and energy requirements of the species, this is not grossly disproportionate to its needs (Ehrlich, 1986). On the other hand, the denial of 40 per cent of NPP to the other species of the earth – and primarily the other higher organisms – is at the source of the problem of biological diversity. The other 5 to 10 million species cannot be expected to survive on only half of the earth's product, when they have been accustomed to a far greater share over the course of evolution.

The source of the problem, then, is the amount of wastage which humans generate in the process of consuming NPP. In the long run it will be necessary to achieve some sort of constraint on the amount of direct use of ecosystem product; however, in the short run it is necessary to remove this high level of indirect use in order to avoid imminent mass extinctions. In addition, this points to the manner in which development might be compatible with the maintenance of biological diversity. In short, it should be possible to maintain or even increase current levels of direct use of NPP, while simultaneously increasing the amount of resources allowed to other species. All that is required is an overhaul of our methods of production in order to reduce the massive amounts of waste and indirect use currently within the system.

The Conversion of Natural Habitat – Addressing the Problem

To address the problem of indirect use and waste of NPP, it is important to understand the system which encourages this manner of production. The modern method of agriculture has itself been developed in response to economic forces; in particular, it is the result of the application of the law of specialization to the countryside.

The law of specialization is one of the first and most important principles of economics. In its crudest form it states that if an individual undertakes the same task many times – i.e. specializes – that person will be more productive than if he or she had undertaken to do the same number of different tasks. Adam Smith first discussed this principle in the context of an early factory in which the breakdown of manufacturing into a number of discrete tasks performed repeatedly was capable of vastly outperforming a single individual attempting to perform all the tasks alone. Obviously, the principle caught hold and is currently the basis for most of production in the Western world.

There is a clear trade-off between productivity and variety in the principle of specialization. Although these factories are capable of producing vastly greater quantities, they do so at the expense of reducing each individual's task to an unvaryingly routine one. In addition, larger factories and more specialization can further reduce costs, resulting in a large price differential between goods produced by this method and those produced in accordance with an individual's order, i.e. "hand crafted". Therefore, there is a loss of variety in the tasks performed and the goods produced in accordance with the force of specialization.

Specialization came to the countryside long ago. Settled agriculture of the Western variety has usually involved the clearing of the natural habitat for replacement by one or a few cultivated species. Such monocultural production has great advantages in terms of specialization, but obviously reduces the diversity of the produce.

Specialization in agricultural production confers productivity gains by virtue of doing repeated tasks – that is, it is easier to plant a field in one crop than in several. In addition, the homogeneity of the crop allows the owner to invest in capital goods which are able to do a single task much more quickly and capably than a human; for example, converting a piece of land to the production of a single crop allows the use of machinery for planting and harvesting, and the use of chemicals which are capable of targeting all competitors ("pests") for the chosen crop. These gains to agricultural specialization have long been known as the initial steps along the road of Western-style development.

It is this process of *conversion* from heterogeneous production to specialized homogeneous production which is largely responsible for the looming biological diversity crisis. As with any process of specialization, the gains in productivity have come at the expense of losses in variety. There are fewer than two dozen species which figure prominently in international trade (FAO 1988a).

In addition, this manner of production is largely responsible for the high levels of human indirect use of NPP, because specialized production requires the removal of much habitat which would otherwise "get in the way" of mass production – trees and brush, for example, are often cleared or burnt. Furthermore, specialized production often hinges upon human appropriation of a larger share of a smaller product from the ecosystem. For example, most crop production results in a large quantity of edible (by some species) matter, of which humans usually take only the fruit or seeds for direct consumption (e.g. maize kernels, roots of certain crops); nevertheless, the entirety of the crop is withheld from these other species in order to protect the small proportion directly consumed. Ultimately much of this biomass is returned directly to the earth without being used by a higher organism, and this is the primary contributing factor to the high rate of human use of ecosystem services. Therefore, the gains in labour productivity have often come at the expense of disproportionate withdrawals of these resources from the use of other species.

The global impact of the force of specialization in agricultural production is easily demonstrated. The losses of variety are staggering: of the thousands of species of plants which are deemed edible and adequate substitutes for human consumption, there are now only twenty which produce the vast majority of the world's food (Vietmeyer, 1986). In fact, the four big carbohydrate crops (wheat, rice, maize and potatoes) feed more people than the next twenty-six crops combined. (Witt, 1985).

In the developed countries of Europe and the USA, the force of specialization has largely completed its task. The proportion of Europe which is now natural habitat (at least 4000 sq. km. in area) is certifiably zero. In the USA, a mere 500 years after the

---

Box 10.3 Rates of Conversion of Natural Habitat to Agriculture

During the past three decades the developing countries have been pursuing a strategy of rapidly converting natural habitat to agricultural production. This process has been largely completed in the developed world; the amount of certifiable natural habitat remaining there is less than 1 per cent (compared with 39 per cent worldwide). Therefore, little conversion continues to occur in the developed world.

Developing	1960 ha	1980 ha	Percent. Change %
Sub-S Africa	161 m	222 m	37.8
Latin America	104 m	142 m	36.5
South Asia	153 m	210 m	37.2
SE Asia	40 m	55 m	37.5
Developed			
North America	205 m	203 m	0.1
Europe	151 m	137 m	−10.0
USSR	225 m	233 m	2.0

Source: R. Repetto and M. Gillis (eds) (1988), *Public Policies and the Misuse of Forest Resources*, Cambridge University Press, Cambridge.

---

introduction of the first Europeans, the proportion of natural habitat of this dimension is now down to 5 per cent (World Resources Institute, 1990). These figures may be compared to a worldwide average of 39 per cent of all territory which remains undeveloped.

At the existing margin, the process of conversion continues at a rapid pace. Although there remains little land to convert to specialized production in the developed countries, the developing countries have adopted and implemented this strategy with real enthusiasm over the past thirty years, often at the urging of development banks.

These rates of conversion of natural habitat represent region-wide rates of increases of agricultural lands of over 17

Box 10.4   Recent Rates of Conversion to Agriculture

The general rates of conversion between 1960 and 1980 were very high (in excess of 17 per cent) as the doctrine of classical development was implemented across wide ranges of the developing world. Rates of increase even in excess of these rates still continue in certain areas of the world; many of them those which harbour the vast majority of remaining biological diversity, i.e. the tropical forested nations.

Conversions to Cropland			*Conversions to Pastureland*	
1.	Paraguay	71.2%	1. Ecuador	61.5%
2.	Niger	32.0%	2. Costa Rica	34.1%
3.	Mongolia	31.9%	3. Thailand	32.1%
4.	Brazil	22.7%	4. Philippines	26.2%
5.	Ivory Cst	22.4%	5. Paraguay	26.0%
6.	Uganda	21.4%	6. Vietnam	14.0%
7.	Guyana	21.3%	7. Nicaragua	11.8%
8.	Burkina F.	19.4%		
9.	Rwanda	18.6%		
10.	Thailand	17.1%		

Source: World Resources Institute and International Institute for Environment and Development (1990), *World Resources 1990–91*, Earthscan, London.

per cent per decade. Recently, these rates have declined somewhat (14.1 per cent for South America; 4.6 per cent for Africa in the decade to 1987); however, the current rates of increase exceed even the rates of the previous two decades in certain areas. In many cases, these areas are precisely at the core of the remaining areas of substantial amounts of biological diversity.

In sum, the problem of biological diversity is largely attributable to the losses in natural habitat. In turn, these losses of natural habitat are occurring because of the process of converting these lands to specialized production. Specialized production is one of the hallmarks of Western-style development, but it implies substantial losses of diversity whenever it is applied. To address the basic causes of biodiversity losses will require the in-depth examination of this link between development and specialized production, and the conversion of natural habitat which it implies in the agricultural context. Conversions from heterogeneous and diverse means of production ("natural habitat production") to homogeneous and single-species production ("specialized agricultural production") has been an assumed necessary step along the path to development. This need not be true, even if it has been true in the past.

The Case Against Continuing Natural Habitat Conversions

There is substantial evidence accumulating which indicates that the financial returns to following the classical path to development – and especially specialized agricultural production – are declining rapidly. For example, despite the fact that developing countries have converted substantial amounts of formerly natural habitat to the production of traditional agricultural commodities, these countries have realized no relative increase in value from these conversions – that is to say, although the value of their production of these commodities has increased, it has not increased any more than the value of the production of the developed countries (who have not converted any natural habitat in the same period).

Box 10.5   **The Value of Converting Natural Habitat**

During the past few decades the developing countries have increased the proportion of their lands dedicated to specialized agricultural production by substantial percentages, while the developed countries have not. In spite of this, the increase in the value of production of these agricultural commodities has been almost equal in the two regions. There has been no relative return to the increased rates of conversion.

Region	Conversion to Agriculture	Increase in Value
LDCS	37% increase	24% increase
DCS	No change	21% increase

Source: M. Holdgate, M. Kassas, and G. White (eds) (1982), *The World Environment 1972–1982*, United Nations Environment Programme, Nairobi.

A general explanation for this trend is the absence of significant demand for the additional quantities of the same commodities. Specialized agricultural production has been constructed around the mass production of large quantities of a few basic commodities. Capital goods, chemicals and techniques have all been geared towards a very small number of plant and animal species. Mass production requires the sacrificing of variety in the pursuit of cost savings, and agricultural specialization has focused on meeting the demand for a small number of basic commodities that are in substantial demand by most of the world's consumers.

However, Western production already goes a long way towards completely satisfying this demand. Further production of these already overproduced commodities will only result in depressing their prices. This is an example of what economists know as operating on the *inelastic* portion of the demand curve for a given commodity. In essence, price inelasticity means that further quantities of the good on the market will necessitate more than proportional reductions in the price in order to dispose of them. The net effect is that more production results in lost revenues.

Some studies of commodity production in the less developed countries have reported this effect in practice. For example, in Sub-Saharan Africa 60 per cent of export earnings come from commodities for which the price elasticity of demand in the West is such that an increase in production of those commodities would actually reduce earnings (Godfrey, 1985). This pattern, however, is much more general than a specific example demonstrates. In fact, the general index of commodity prices has fallen by 50 per cent over the past thirty years, the same period in which the majority of conversions to specialized agricultural production have occurred.

Overall, classical development policies have not worked well for a large portion of the developing world, in particular for those countries focusing on the development of production in the traditional export commodities. While agricultural produc-

---

Box 10.6 The Trend in the Prices of Traditional Commodities

The reason for the absence of a financial return to the conversion of natural habitat is the effect of increased production the prices of these commodities. Most of them have long been in surplus on the world's markets, and thus increases in supply result in further falls in the relative price of the good. Over the past thirty years, the real value of the traditional commodities has fallen by nearly 50%

Year	Commodities Price Index (1960 = 100)
1960	100
1965	95
1970	91
1975	105 (impact of oil cartel)
1980	85
1985	65
1987	62

Source: International Monetary Fund (1988), *World Economic Outlook 1988*, Washington, DC.

tion in the developing countries has skyrocketed by virtue of the conversion of large quantities of previously natural habitat (1960–80: Africa 35 per cent, Latin America 75 per cent, South Asia 45 per cent), there has been no corresponding increase in the value of this production. To a large extent, these countries have chosen to follow an already too well trodden path towards development, and there is no longer any room in the market at the end of that road.

The Value of Natural Habitat Production

There are two specific reasons why the value of the goods and services which flow from natural habitats might be expected to exceed its converted value. The first is the relative scarcity value of natural habitat, and hence its products. The second is the increased NPP of natural habitat.

As conversions of natural habitat have occurred, the remaining stock has been irretrievably reduced. This means that the obvious sources of supply of the unique products of natural habitat have been diminished. This points unambiguously to an increase in the price of such goods and services. At the same time, the amount of land dedicated to traditional agricultural commodity production has increased, thereby reducing the relative value of these commodities. The dynamics of this process indicate that the comparative advantage of natural habitat production must have been increasing throughout the past three decades, and that it would be predictable that in some instances the financial returns from the use of the products of natural habitat would now exceed the value of the products of the land if it were to be converted.

A number of studies have demonstrated precisely this effect. The use of natural habitat for wildlife products (hunting, skins, ivory, etc.) in Zimbabwe has been demonstrated to be the best use of those lands in that country. In Kenya, the use of natural habitat for the purpose of wildlife tourism far exceeds its alternative use value. Cattle ranching in Brazil and Peru has been demonstrated to be an inferior use of converted rainforest. Similarly, in Malaysia, the transfer of rainforest to

Box 10.7 **The Comparative Value of Natural Habitat Production**

A number of studies have demonstrated that the value of the product of natural habitat is greater than the value of its product if it were to be converted to another use.

Country	Natural Habitat Use & Value	Alternative Use & Value
Kenya	Wildlife Tourism (much higher)	Cattle Ranching
Zimbabwe	Wildlife Production Z\$4.20/ha	Cattle Ranching Z\$3.58/ha
Malaysia	Forest Production \$2455/ha	Intensive Agric. \$217/ha
Peru	Forest Production \$6820/ha	Clear-cut \$1000/ha

Sources: Zimbabwe – Child (1984); Kenya – Western (1984); Malysia – Watson (1988); Peru – Peters et al. (1989).

intensive cultivation was found to result in a substantial net loss in value.

Each of these studies demonstrates that the value of the products of natural habitats exceeds the value of the land if converted to traditional agricultural commodity production. In Zimbabwe, that value is captured by marketing products from elephants (ivory and skins) and other game animals as well as by allowing local communities to utilize the thatch grown within the reserves. In Malysia, the natural habitat products include rattan and fuelwood. In Peru, the products are primarily fruits and latex, with some selective logging and fuelwood use.

These examples demonstrate the value of the diversity of uses that natural habitat production can supply. Clearly, natural habitats can produce game for food and commodities for trade. In addition, a primary source of energy throughout much of the developing world is fuelwood, a major proportion of which comes from natural habitat (Prescott-Allan and Prescott-Allan, 1982). Even the materials necessary for dwellings are provided by natural habitat: the value of the thatch harvest from Royal Chitwan National Park in Nepal exceeds \$600,000 annually (Mishra, 1984). In Venezuela, it has been found that the designation of a high-altitude national park was sufficient to ensure high-quality water supplies from that watershed (Garcia, 1984). Therefore, one of the important characteristics of natural habitats is the sheer variety of uses which it can generate: food, energy, building materials, exchangeable commodities – even water supplies.

Some of the value of natural habitat production is already being attained, but is unaccounted for in national accounts and decision-making. For example, many indigenous peoples depend for their very survival on the value of natural habitat production. Estimates of regional reliance upon "game meat" exceed 80 per cent in Peru, and 70 per cent throughout rural Ghana (Ajayi, 1979; Sale, 1981). A large proportion of states take a substantial amount of their animal protein from natural habitats. Many times these products of natural habitats do not pass through a market, because they are used directly by local communities and hence are not given a specific value in the process; however, it is fundamentally important that this

---

Box 10.8 **Unaccounted-for Value of Natural Habitat Production**

Many people currently use natural habitats as a primary source of their food supplies. Much of this produce is consumed directly, and is never taken into consideration as the produce of the natural habitat. It is essential that the subsistence value of natural habitat production be considered in making conversion decisions.

Average Percentage of Animal Protein	*Number of States*
20–29	15
30–39	17
40–49	12
50+	19

Source: R. Prescott-Allan and C. Prescott-Allan (1982), *What's Wildlife Worth?*, Earthscan, London.

production be given its correct valuation in national accounts, and in determinations concerning land use.

Very probably, the greatest earning power of natural habitat in the future lies not in its capacity to produce unique goods, but instead in its capacity to produce unique services. International tourism has been one of the world's growth industries for the past two decades; it has increased tenfold during that period. It now represents 5 per cent of all international trade (World Tourism Organization, 1990).

In the developed world the recreational value of the natural habitat that remains dwarfs the produce value of that same habitat. For example, the value of the Great Lakes as a source of recreation (for fishing purposes) was determined to be $500 million in 1984, while the value of the fish taken was only $6 million (Robinson and Bolen, 1989). Similarly, in the Scottish salmon fisheries, sports fishing clubs have recently been buying out the fishing rights of long-standing commercial fishing companies (Luxmoore and Swanson, 1991).

In the developing world, the value of ecotourism is also rising against the other uses of remaining natural habitat. For example, in several of the tropically forested states – Costa Rica, Ecuador, the Philippines and Thailand – tourism ranks among the top five industries and brings in more foreign exchange than timber sales. Similarly, in Africa, wildlife-related tourism is a substantial generator of export earnings (30 per cent in Kenya; $6 million for hunting licences alone in Zimbabwe).

The goods and services of natural habitats are limited to the remaining unaltered habitat, which is always dwindling in size. For this reason, the comparative value of these products is increasing. Just as importantly, natural habitat production has the additional advantage of increasing the ratio of direct to indirect use of a given piece of land. That is, production of goods in the context of a natural habitat implies the minimum intervention required for their production, and hence the minimum amount of indirect use of resources in the production process. This is ultimately the way in which development can be unlinked from diversity destruction. If the direct use of a given ecosystem's produce can be increased, even substantially, while simultaneously decreasing the indirect use, then it is possible to have growth in combination with the preservation of diversity.

As noted above, the current rate of human use of NPP is 40 per cent, but 36 per cent of this use is indirect or wastage. If production occurred in the context of natural habitats rather than specialized agriculture, it would be possible to have substantial increases in the proportion of NPP consumed by humans, while still making greater portions of NPP available to other species as well (since indirect use and wastage could then be substantially reduced). Following the classic path to development cannot accomplish this objective, as its indirect use requirements (26 per cent of NPP) are too high to be compatible with significant amounts of biological diversity. Natural habitat production is the method by which development and diversity might be linked; this is the real value of this method of production.

Use It or Lose It

To many, the concept of natural habitat utilization will seem antithetical to the entire idea of natural habitat conservation. That is, from this "preservationist" perspective, the value of the natural habitat is lost once any manner of human intervention occurs.

This is a reasonable position if you are a European, or of European derivation, given the history of Western involvement with nature. Once Europeans have entered into an area, the process of specialization in use has seldom been long in coming. However, other cultures have not been so determined to make use of their environment by initially "clearing the slate", and many of these peoples have managed to live within their environment with a much lower level of intervention. To presume that they would be unable to balance use and preservation is largely arguing against their historical record.

Natural habitats are largely unprotected still, and all of them are subject to the forces for conversion. Their maintenance at anything like existing levels will require the demonstration of their value. Minimally necessary intervention, for the purposes of harvesting or generating greater productivity, will be a necessary component of a strategy of natural habitat maintenance.

Intervention for the purpose of sustainable harvests of natural habitat production is an obvious component of a strategy of optimal utilization. Intervention at earlier stages for the purpose of increasing those harvests is more controversial, but an equally important part of such a programme. For example, in the "ranching" of some lizards it has been discovered that intervention at the egg-laying stage can reduce infant mortality from 95 per cent to 5 per cent, with a modest investment in egg collection and incubation equipment. Hence, a productivity gain of about 1800 per cent is achievable by means of intervention at this stage, with the subsequent release of the animals back into the natural habitat after hatching (Nelson, 1986). Similar productivity gains may be achievable with regard to many reptiles by the use of such methods.

Intervention might occur at any of a number of stages in the development of a harvestable species: breeding, infancy, juvenilehood, harvestable adult. The correct calculation would weigh the benefits against the costs of the withdrawal of the species from the natural habitat during each of the above periods. For example, once again regarding reptiles, the productivity gains for intervention at the stage of infancy are substantial enough to warrant the removal of the lizards from the natural habitat then, but at no other stage until harvest. For crocodiles, on the other hand, it pays to leave a breeding population in the wild, while taking eggs for hatching and development until the time of harvesting (in juvenilehood).

In this way, these two species are contributing in their own ways to the appropriation of the value of their natural habitats, and hence to the maintenance of those habitats. Some species of lizard can do this by eating the leaves of tropical trees, rather than the commercial feeds that would otherwise be necessary, and turning those leaves into ultimately valuable meat, eggs and skins. Crocodiles do this by inhabiting and using tropical wetlands and rivers, and contributing an annual clutch of eggs as their payment in kind. These eggs are then developed by factory methods into crocodile skins and meat.

These interventions are ultimately necessary as the means of appropriating the value of the natural habitat through the mechanism of these individual species. Although it is not a purist solution, it is probably the only possible solution. The development of more and better mechanisms for capturing the value of natural habitat will be fundamental to its maintenance. From this perspective, it is better to make some use of this natural habitat than to lose it all.

Problems to be Solved in Natural Habitat Maintenance

There are several important problems which stand as significant hurdles to the maintenance of remaining natural habitat. The first is the nature of some of the important products of natural habitat (primarily information), which are very difficult to value. The second is the nature of the ownership structure (common) for natural habitats, which is generally difficult to implement effectively. Finally, there is the problem of conflicting uses: the difficulty of obtaining the value of one use without seriously reducing that of another. The nature of each of these problems will be described briefly here in order to indicate the scale of the difficulties that must be overcome, if the object of natural habitat maintenance is to be achieved.

Many of the goods and services of natural habitats are of the nature of so-called "collective goods" – that is, these products are beneficial not to a particular user, but rather to a broad swathe of humanity. One of the primary attributes of natural habitat is the untapped information which it represents. For example, there are at present 119 plant-derived drugs in use throughout the world, obtained from fewer than 90 species of plant (Farnsworth, 1986), yet there are about 250,000 to 750,000 species of plants still to be tested. There is a substantial value to be placed on the maintenance of this stock of potential information, but the benefit is largely for all.

Similarly, the value of the variety which exists in the wild is also of importance for the improvement of domestic species. The discovery of a naturally virus-resistant species of wild maize (teosinte) in Mexico in 1979 was of potential billion-dollar importance to the domestic species; yet when its importance was discovered, all that remained of the species was a six-hectare patch high on the Sierra de Manantlan. This is a simple but laborious process of collecting species and then undertaking careful analysis of their differences; for example, the collection of a species of wild tomato in the Andes in 1963 resulted, after ten generations of crossing with the domestic species, in a marked commercial improvement valued at about $8 million per annum (Iltis, 1986).

Natural habitat represents a library of such information, but the value of that information accrues to all, and is not likely to be considered by any one individual when deciding whether to convert the habitat. This indicates the difference between financial analysis and economic analysis: the latter states that even when individuals do not take real value into account, systems must be created which do.

Other collective benefits of natural habitat are equally difficult to value through ordinary mechanisms. For example, forested habitat often plays an important role in both the maintenance of watersheds and the fixing of carbon, as was discussed in an earlier chapter. These values must also be taken into account in determining the amount of natural habitat that must be maintained.

Finally, the mere existence of habitat is of significant value. This is indicated in part by the fact that individuals are willing to contribute money to organizations whose stated objective is the preservation of natural habitat and wild species. For example, in 1990 the donated budgets of the National Wildlife Federation and the World Wide Fund for Nature were $100 million and $50 million, respectively.

The first hurdle to the maintenance of significant quantities of natural habitat is the creation of mechanisms which are capable of capturing some of these less tangible, but equally important, values. The maximum amount of habitat can be maintained only if all this value is captured.

The second hurdle to be crossed involves the nature of the management of natural habitats. Usually, natural habitat will require a significant amount of land to be held in an undivided state; interventions (e.g. fencing) which subdivide natural habitat usually lead to extinctions. The management of parcels of natural habitat of substantial size is a difficult proposition because it is not easy to ensure that all users are acting in common interest. Much of the activity in natural habitat is currently being undertaken on an unsustainable basis, to the detriment of all users, precisely because it is undertaken in natural habitat. Although not impossible, this is a substantial hurdle to overcome. The first step is the enlistment of local community efforts in the management of the habitat, which is most easily acquired by making the community the first appropriators of the value of the habitat, i.e. the "owners".

Finally, it is important to note that in some cases it will be difficult to sum up all the values of natural habitat, simply because some of them are mutually exclusive. That is, some uses (e.g. more non-consumptive uses such as wildlife tourism) are not very compatible with others (e.g. more consumptive uses such as game hunting). It will be necessary to make the right choices with regard to any particular piece of habitat, in order to maximize its particular value and therefore its chances of survival.

Therefore, the maintenance of natural habitats through their utilization is itself fraught with difficulties, but attention must now be turned to the solution of these problems, not their avoidance. There is no alternative, other than the exhaustion of this ancient resource. We must take actions which will give the remaining natural habitat at least a chance of long-term survival, in the most unmodified state possible.

References

Ajayi, S. (1979), *Utilization of Forest Wildlife in West Africa*, Rome: FAO.

Bell, R. and E. McShane-Caluzi (eds) (1984), *Conservation and Wildlife Management in Africa*, Washington, DC: US Peace Corps.

Berkes, F. (ed.) (1989), *Common Property Resources: Ecology and Community Based Sustainable Development*, London: Belhaven.

Browder, J. (1988), "Public Policy and Deforestation in the Brazilian Amazon", in R. Repetto and M. Gillis (eds), op. cit.

Child, G. (1984), "Managing Wildlife for People in Zimbabwe", in J. McNeely and K. Miller (eds), op. cit.

Child, G. and B. Child (1991), "An Historical Perspective on Sustainable Wildlife Utilization", in *Proceedings of the IUCN Workshop on Wildlife Utilization*, Gland: IUCN.

Ehrlich, P. and A. Ehrlich (1981), *Extinction. The Causes of the Disappearance of Species*, New York: Random House.

Ehrlich, P. (1986), "The Loss of Diversity: Causes and Consequences", in E. O. Wilson (ed.), op. cit.

Eltringham, S. (1984), *Wildlife Resources and Economic Development*, New York: John Wiley.

Farnsworth, N. (1986), "Screening Plants for New Medicines", in E.O. Wilson (ed.), op. cit.

FAO (1980), *Production, Consumption and Trade of Minor Meats – Trends, Prospects and Development Issues*, Rome.

FAO (1988a), *Yearbook of Forest Products*, Rome.

FAO (1988b), *Yearbook of Fishery Statistics*, Rome.

Gadgil, M. and P. Iyer (1988), "On the Diversification of Common Property Resource Use in Indian Society", in F. Berkes (ed.), op. cit.

Garcia, J. (1984), "Waterfalls, Hydropower, and Water for Industry: Contributions from Canaima National Park", in J. McNeely and K. Miller (eds), op. cit.

Gillis, M. (1988), "Indonesia: Public Policies, Resource Management, and the Tropical Forest", in R. Repetto and M. Gillis (eds), op. cit.

Godfrey, M. (1985), in T. Rose (ed.), *Crisis and Recovery in Sub-Saharan Africa*, Paris: OECD.

Holdgate, M., M. Kassas and G. White (eds) (1982), *The World Environment 1972–1982*, Nairobi: United Nations Environment Programme.

Iltis, H. (1986), "Serendipity in the Exploration of Biodiversity", in E.O. Wilson (ed.), op. cit.

International Institute for Environment and Development and World Resources Institute (1989), *World Resources 1988–89*, New York: Basic Books.

International Monetary Fund (1987), *International Financial Statistics*, Washington, DC.

International Monetary Fund (1988), *World Economic Outlook 1988*, Washington, DC.

Kiss, A (ed.) (1990), *Living With Wildlife*, draft report of World Bank Environment Division, Washington, DC: World Bank.

Lovejoy, T. (1980), "A Projection of Species Extinctions", in G.O.

Barney (ed.), *The Global 2000 Report to the President. Entering the Twenty-First Century*, Washington, DC: Council on Environmental Quality.

Lugo, A. (1986), "Estimating Reductions in the Diversity of Tropical Forest Species", in E.O. Wilson (ed.), op. cit.

Luxmoore, R. (1989), "Impact on Conservation", in R. Hudson, K. Drew and L. Baskin (eds), *Wildlife Production Systems: Economic Utilization of Wild Ungulates*, Cambridge: Cambridge University Press.

Luxmoore, R. and T. Swanson (1991), "The Impact of Domestication on the Remaining Wild Populations of a Species – The Case of the Scottish Salmon Fisheries".

MacKinnon, J., K. MacKinnon, G. Child and J. Thorsell (1986), *Managing Protected Areas in the Tropics*, Gland: International Union for the Conservation of Nature.

Martin, R. (1984), "Wildlife Utilization", in R. Bell and E. McShane-Vicuzi (eds), op. cit.

McNeely, J. and K. Miller (eds) (1984), *National Parks, Conservation and Development*, Washington, DC: Smithsonian Institution.

Mishra, H. (1984), "A Delicate Balance: Tigers, Rhinoceros, Tourists and Park Management vs. The Needs of the Local People in Royal Chitwan National Park, Nepal", in J. McNeely and K. Miller (eds), op. cit.

Mittermeier, R. (1986), "Primate Diversity and the Tropical Forest", in E.O. Wilson (ed.), op. cit.

Myers, N. (1979), *The Sinking Ark. A Look at the Problem of Disappearing Species*. New York: Pergamon.

Myers, N. (1983), *A Wealth of Wild Species*, Boulder: Westview.

Myers, N. (1984), *The Primary Source*, New York: Norton.

Nelson, L. (1986), "Economic Analysis of Iguana Ranching", unpublished manuscript.

Norton, B. (ed.) (1986), *The Preservation of Species*, Princeton, NJ: Princeton University Press.

Office of Technology Assessment (1984): Technologies to Sustain Tropical Forest Resources, Washington, DC: US Government Printing Office.

Parker, I. (1984), "Perspectives on Wildlife Cropping or Culling", in R. Bell and E. McShane-Vicuzi (eds), op. cit.

Peters, C., Gentry, A. and Mendelsohn, R. (1989), "Valuation of an Amazonian Rainforest" in *Nature*, vol. 339, p. 665.

Plotkin, M. (1986), "The Outlook for New Agricultural and Industrial Products from the Tropics", in E.O. Wilson (ed.), op. cit.

Prescott-Allan, R. and C. Prescott-Allan (1982), *What's Wildlife*

Worth?, London: Earthscan.

Raup, D. (1986), "Diversity Crises in the Geological Past", in E.O. Wilson (ed.), op. cit.

Repetto, R. (ed.) (1985), *The Global Possible*, New Haven: Yale University Press.

Repetto, R. (1986), "Soil Loss and Population Pressure on Java", Ambio, vol. 15, p. 14.

Repetto, R. and M. Gillis (eds) (1988), *Public Policies and the Misuse of Forest Resources*, Cambridge: Cambridge University Press.

Robinson, W. and E. Bolen (1989), *Wildlife Ecology and Management*, (2nd edn), New York: Macmillan.

Sale, J. (1981), *The Importance and Values of Wild Plants and Animals in Africa*, Gland: International Union for the Conservation of Nature.

Simberloff, D. (1986), "Are We on the Verge of a Mass Extinction in Tropical Rain Forests?", in D.K. Elliot (ed.), *Dynamics of Extinction*, New York: John Wiley and Sons.

Swanson, T. (1991), "The Environmental Economics of Wildlife Utilization", in *Proceedings of the* IUCN *Workshop on Wildlife Utilization*, Gland: IUCN.

Terborgh, J. (1974), "Preservation of Natural Diversity: The Problem of Extinction-Prone Species", *Bioscience*, 24: pp. 715–22.

Thomsen, J. and R. Luxmoore, R. (1991), "Sustainable Utilization of Wildlife for Trade", in *Proceedings of the* IUCN *Workshop on Wildlife Utilization*, Gland: IUCN.

Vietmeyer, N. (1986), "Lesser Known Plants of Potential Use in Agriculture and Forestry", *Science*, 232: pp. 1179–1384.

Vitousek, P., P. Ehrlich, A. Ehrlich and P. Matson (1986), "Human Appropriation of the Products of Photosynthesis", *Bioscience*, vol. 36, no. 6, pp. 368–73.

Watson, D. (1988), "The Evolution of Appropriate Resource Management Systems", in F. Berkes (ed.), op. cit.

Western, D. (1984), "Amboseli National Park: Human Values and the Conservation of a Savanna Ecosystem", in J. McNeely and K. Miller (eds), op. cit.

Wilson, E.O. (ed.) (1986), *Biodiversity*, Washington, DC: National Academy.

Wilson, E.O. (1986a), "The Current State of Biological Diversity", in E. Wilson (ed.), op. cit.

Witt, S. (1985), *Biotechnology and Genetic Diversity*, San Fransisco: California Agricultural Lands Project.

World Bank (1989), *World Development Report*, Oxford: Oxford Univ. Press.

World Resources Institute and International Institute for Environment and Development (1990), *World Resources 1990–91*, London: Earthscan.

World Tourism Organization (WTO) (1990), *World Tourism and Travel Statistics*, New York.

Yeager, R. and N. Miller (1986), *Wild Life, Wild Death*, Albany, NJ: State University of New York.

11

Environment, Economics and Ethics

R. Kerry Turner

Introduction

"Sustainable development" has become a catch-all phrase for forms of economic development which stress the importance of environmental quality and the conservation of nature's assets.[1] Definitions of sustainable development abound, and some analysts worry that if sustainability eludes formal definition, it cannot serve as a basis for formulating appropriate environmental policy. Alternatively, it has also been argued that it is not sustainability that requires definition or clarification, but rather the context in which it is set. Sustainability thinking is usually used to modify the context to which it is applied. It serves to highlight unsustainable systems and resource management practices. There is also an underlying assumption that sustainability is desirable — it is a policy objective we ought to seek to achieve. In other words, deep questions of ethics and morality are involved in the sustainability debate.

The sustainability concept, regardless of its definitional problems, can play a catalytic role as a means of exploring the interface between environmental economics, environmental science and ethics. The purpose of this chapter is to provide a rudimentary appreciation of the ethical perspective as it affects sustainability issues.

The increasing level of general environmental awareness over the last few decades has served to highlight the "narrowness" of conventional economic analysis. In particular, environmentalists (and some economists) have been critical of what they see as the increasingly strained application of conventional economics (as illustrated by cost-benefit analysis) to sustainability issues such as the transportation and storage of highly toxic and long-lived waste, man-induced climate change and biodiversity loss. Concern has been expressed about the adequacy, in these applications, of the conceptual and empirical basis of economics. Difficult questions of valuation, fairness and compensation readily come to the surface and greatly complicate policy-making and its supporting analysis.

The rise of environmentalism (as a social and political movement) since the 1960s has also led to a renewed interest by some philosophers in applied moral philosophy. As yet there is no consensus among philosophers as to whether an environmental ethic can be given rational and theoretical support, or what the content of the ethic should be. In principle, the aim would be to formulate agreed codes of conduct regulating human behaviour towards nature. We may, however, have to settle for something less. Environmental ethics may turn out to be no more than an account of various kinds of ethical theories set in the context of environmental problem issues. Some of the more radical philosophical ideas would have significant implications for environmental economics, for sustainable development strategies and sustainable systems themselves.

The Brundtland Commission[2] defined sustainable development as: ". . . development that meets the needs of the present without compromising the ability of future generations to meet their own needs" (p. 43). An economic interpretation of this concept would be that the welfare of people alive today should not be increased by development activity if as a consequence the welfare of future generations would be reduced. Economists are familiar with this as the Pareto criterion for establishing an increase in the overall welfare of society. The Pareto rule would approve (i.e. judge it to be a contribution to increased economic efficiency) of a policy, programme or project if it succeeded in making some people better off without making anyone else worse off.

In practical cost-benefit analysis (CBA) the Pareto criterion is modified in order to incorporate the idea of potential compensation. This is because in the real world very few projects/policies result in gains and no losses. In the majority of cases where there are winners and losers from a project or policy change, economists adopt the Potential Pareto criterion in order to pronounce on the economic efficiency implications. They therefore judge that there is an increase in potential welfare if those who gain from a project/policy could, hypothetically, compensate those who lose.

The idea of potential welfare is not consistent with the sustainability objective because the latter is partly an equity-orientated goal. Sustainable development requires that both equity and efficiency objectives are served through actual compensation:

(a) by gainers now to losers now – intragenerational compensation; and
(b) by gainers now to losers in the future – intergenerational compensation.

In the next sections we examine alternative approaches for choosing between environmental resource conservation and economic development, and emphasize the ethical concerns involved. The discussion is focused on project/policy appraisal procedures as elements of an overall environmental management strategy (world-view). Since 1970 four basic world views have crystallized within environmentalism, although this categorization should not be interpreted as a series of watertight compartments – in reality the positions overlap, and a large number of combined positions are possible. Simplifying matters a great deal, the four positions are:

a resource-exploitative, growth-orientated world-view;
a resource-conservationist, managed growth world-view;
a resource-preservationist, severely constrained growth world-view; and
an extreme resource-preservationist, zero-growth world-view.[3]

Philosophers have continued to debate whether an entirely new environmental ethic is required, or alternatively whether traditional forms of ethical reasoning need supplementing or revision. Even this latter position is not a uniform stance, as philosophers debate the limits to the extensiveness of any revision or modification of traditional ethics.

Given the complexity and wide range of philosophical ideas involved in the debate, this chapter will be restricted to an outline of three ethical issues that seem to lie at the heart of the environmental ethics controversy. Different approaches to environmental resource management will therefore be distinguished in terms of whether a human-centred (anthropocentric) or nature-centred (ecocentric) world-view is adopted. The notion of distributional equity will also be examined; finally, the concept of environmental value and its expression will be investigated.

Alternative Approaches to Environmental Resource Management

Four main approaches to project appraisal and resource management have emerged over the last few decades as environmentalism has gained ground:

(1) Conventional CBA framework (exploitationist world-view)

In this approach, conventional CBA is retained as a narrow measure of the economic efficiency of alternative projects and/or courses of action. CBA is based on a utilitarian ethical system which sets the ground rules for the comparison of gains and losses. This version of utilitarianism requires that the individual person maximize only their own well-being (utility). Under certain very restrictive conditions this can result in a welfare maximum for the whole economic system, for a given distribution of income and wealth. Ethically the aim would be to maximize net total utility, ignoring the significance of the resulting distribution of gains and losses, so in this approach it does not matter who in a particular society gets the benefits or who bears the costs. Equity considerations are therefore just not addressed explicitly at all.

The environment is viewed as a collection of goods and

services and is of instrumental value to humans – i.e. nature is valuable because humans use it, directly or indirectly, or rely on it for life support. The conventional economic approach is therefore said to be both utilitarian and anthropocentric (human-based).

The value of all environmental assets is assumed to be measured by individuals' preferences for the conservation of those assets. Individuals have a number of held values which in turn result in objects being given various assigned values. Individuals are assumed to express their preferences and valuations by their willingness to pay for goods and services in the marketplace. Many environmental resources are not marketable assets and therefore do not have a market price value assigned to them.[4] There is the prospect, then, that conventional CBA will fail to incorporate the full range of environmental impacts relating to a given development project or policy. The impacts will remain outside the CBA calculus because of its market-value bias and the difficulty of establishing market surrogates.

Environmental impact assessment (EIA) methods and techniques could be used to gain a more comprehensive appreciation of the environmental effects of development activities. EIA produces a quantified but non-monetary assessment of the environmental consequences of a project or policy. It would, however, be viewed as an entirely separate procedure from CBA.

CBA would be conducted on the basis of a discounting procedure with a normal discount rate (positive rates of time preference amongst individuals is assumed) being applied to all projects regardless of the project lifetime and the distribution of costs and benefits over that lifetime. Future-orientated activities in the present would be regarded as investments for the future. Long-run significantly large damage costs associated with a particular project would appear in the discounted project balance sheet as very modest numbers as long as discount rates were positive. Future costs and benefits are given less weight than current costs and benefits, and part of the justification for this procedure is the technocentric/exploitationist world-view that underpins the conventional approach to resource management.

The exploitationist position favours an economic growth ethic. Economic growth provides increasing material benefits, increasing consumer choice and want satisfaction, and therefore more human welfare. Technical fixes and substitution mechanisms can be relied upon to mitigate resource scarcities. Research and development expenditure by the current generation contributes to a stock of human capital (including knowledge) that is inherited by future generations. The implication is that future generations will be richer and better able to cope with any environmental cost burdens they receive from earlier economic activities undertaken by their ancestors.

(2) Modified "extended" CBA *approach (conservationist world-view)*

In this approach, the utilitarian cost-benefit paradigm is relaxed to allow for a concept of intergenerational equity. Sustainable development is seen to involve compensating the future for environmental damage being done now, and damage done in the past. Compensation requires the passing-on to future generations of a stock of natural assets no smaller than the stock in the possession of current generations. This "constant natural assets" requirement produces modifications to the CBA approach, notably by raising the implicit value of environmental impacts relative to "development".

The constant natural assets rule reflects a moral imperative to care for the next generation, and this imperative is not readily interpreted in terms of utilitarian gains and losses. Thus maintaining natural assets is wholly consistent with current generations bearing a cost, say x, which generates benefits for future generations of, say, 0.5x. The utilitarian rule would reject this "trade" because future benefits are less than the current sacrifice. The constant natural assets rule could, however, be consistent with that same "trade", that is to say, current generations may have to bear higher costs than future gains in order to maintain constant natural assets. This modified cost-benefit paradigm therefore allows for non-utilitarian values but retains its anthropocentric bias. The "fairness" in question is fairness between people.

The unease felt by many people about the neglect of the interests of future generations in the current generation's development activities perhaps reflects an intuitive feeling that future generations are both powerless (they have no role in the decision-making process of today) and vulnerable.[5] It is from this awareness that arguments in favour of a stewardship ethic to protect the interests of future generations, or of rights for future generations, have sprung.

But traditional systems of ethics do not in general support the proposition that current generations have moral obligations to future people.[6] Some utilitarian philosophers have stressed the point that future people (as individuals) may not exist at all. In the here and now they are only "possible" people, and their actual number depends in large measure upon current actions and decisions. Current policy therefore cannot be governed by reference to harm to the interests of future individuals, because those policies determine who those individuals will be and what interests they will have. Some utilitarians may conclude that the present generation has no obligations to future people. They would argue that a person has not been wronged by another unless he/she has been made worse off by the other's act. Nothing which we (the current generation) can do can wrong future actual people (brought about by our actions), unless what we do results in such a "poor" future world that these actual future people turn out to wish they had never been born at all.

So what ethical sources do exist which could offer support to the notions of intragenerational and intergenerational equity and related rules like the constant natural assets rule? A number of analysts have turned to contractarian philosophy, and in particular to the work of one ethical philosopher, John Rawls.[7]

In the context of intragenerational justice, Rawls's just society is based on principles chosen by rational and risk-averse individual representatives from contemporary society in an "original position" (the negotiations) and operating from behind what he calls a "veil of ignorance" (i.e. individuals are assumed not to know to which stratum of society they themselves belong). So what, according to Rawls, are the principles of justice that he thinks would be chosen by society behind the veil of ignorance? Two important principles would be equal opportunity for all individuals and the "difference principle" or maximum criterion (i.e. an acceptable standard of living for the least well off in society).

The difference principle could be applied to the current global inequities between the Northern industrialized economies and the poorer developing economies of the South. Since the early 1970s there have been persistent calls from the South for the establishment of a new international economic order. According to the Rawlsian argument, the greater wealth of some nations could be defended if it improved the expectations of the least advantaged countries and did not impair the long-term development of these countries by seriously damaging their environments.[8]

During the early 1980s the Brandt Commission reports (in 1980 and 1983)[9] came close to justifying the international trading system (albeit with some reforms) on this basis. The Brandt reports put forward an economic interdependency thesis buttressed by the supposed existence of mutual and/or common interests between North and South. A central Brandt argument was that in an increasingly interdependent world the opportunities to exploit mutual interest (i.e. objectives pursued by exchange) in the recovery of the international economy should be grasped. The South would gain in terms of increased export revenues and the North could protect large numbers of jobs supposedly dependent on sales markets in the South. There is, however, good reason to doubt the validity of this mutual interest argument. The prospects for export-led growth in the developing countries have proved to be far from uniform. If the prospects of the least fortunate countries are not so enhanced, the global inequality cannot be justified.[10]

A constant or rising natural capital stock (constant natural assets rule) is also likely to serve the goal of intragenerational fairness – i.e. justice to the socially disadvantaged both within any one country and between countries at a given point in time. This is most clearly seen in the context of poor developing countries in which direct dependence on natural resources is paramount. In these countries the "environment–poverty trap" prevails: as poverty increases, natural environments are degraded to obtain immediate food supplies. As environments degrade, so the prospects for future livelihoods decrease. Environmental degradation generates more poverty, thus accelerating the cycle. The provision of natural capital offers one way of breaking into the cycle.

Rawls himself provides only a very limited treatment of the intergenerational equity question. He views it primarily in terms of the present generation's duty to save. A "just" savings rate (constant over time) would be one which improves the lot of each succeeding generation without undue hardship on any earlier generation.[11] A number of analysts find this argument unsatisfactory and have sought to apply the difference principle intertemporally in order to ensure future generations an adequate natural resource endowment and a liveable environment. Attempts have been made to adapt the Rawlsian original position so that the rational choosers did not know which generation they were going to be part of. It is then argued that they would emphasize intergenerational equity for the same reasons that Rawls supposed they would in developing principles of intragenerational justice.[12]

The model of human beings as merely rational, self-interested calculating machines is obviously very restricted and neglects the social and communal aspects of human nature. Humans may therefore possess private and public preferences (as the basis of valuation). The latter preferences relate to what the individual thinks is in the public or community interest. If individuals support such a "collectivist" approach, then so-called "generalized obligations" may exist. These obligations might extend to a feeling that the current generation ought to maintain a stable flow of resources into the future (an inheritance of natural and man-made capital) in order to ensure ongoing human life rather than just meeting individual requirements.

Given a collectivist position, the principle of intergenerational equity has been interpreted as a "justice as opportunity" argument.[13] The presentation of "opportunities" for future generations becomes a minimal notion of intergenerational fairness. The present generation does not have a right to deplete the economic and other opportunities afforded by the resource base (including environmental functions) since it does not "own" it. The passing-on over time of the resource base "intact" does not, however, mean literally physically intact; but when there is depletion, this must be compensated for by technological development or capital investment (e.g. conservation of renewable resources, enhanced technology and recycling innovation).[14]

Once again the constant natural assets rule can help fulfil the intergenerational equity and sustainability objectives. Sustainability and equity can be introduced into the cost-benefit models through the idea of compensating offsets. By analysing an overall portfolio of investments it should be possible to detect the cumulative environmental impact and then identify offsetting environmental improvements. EIA is viewed as a complementary procedure to CBA, providing the necessary database on impacts requiring quantification and eventual evaluation. The modified cost-benefit rule becomes the instrument for achieving constant environmental assets. In turn, constant environmental assets afford protection for future generations and the poor of current generations who depend directly on natural assets.

The modified CBA approach retains its essentially anthropocentric basis and therefore supports an anthropocentric environmental ethic. It highlights the vital sustainable economics principle that natural resources and environments are multifunctional and represent vast storehouses of economic (instrumental) value. The total economic value concept encompasses use, option and existence values.[15] Provided that this value is generally recognized, humans will make arrangements so as adequately to protect their environmental assets.

This anthropocentric line of ethical arguments has proceeded incrementally, gradually moving away from received moral judgements about familiar issues and their consequences and on to analogous cases involving the future for humans. It stops part-way into the non-human realm: it retains the traditional concern for individual beings or accepts a collectivist view of generations of humans but rejects concern for biotic systems as a whole. It is an environmental management ethic based on principles such as stewardship, sustainability and quality of life (for humans today and in the future). Humans should act as nature's stewards and conserve natural resources and the environment, for their own sakes and to protect the interests of other creatures.[16] The constant natural assets rule has an additional protective element in the sense that, conserving critical natural capital on instrumental value and human-based equity grounds, it also conserves the environments of sentient non-humans and non-sentient things.

(3) Radically modified CBA approach (moderate preservationist world-view)

In this approach, economic analysis plays a secondary role to EIA and the process of agreeing and setting pre-emptive environmental standards (e.g. ambient quality standards, conservation zones large enough to sustain important ecosystems, etc). The pre-emptive standards and implied policy priorities are set on the basis of non-economic grounds – i.e. scientific, cultural, historical and ethical. In simplistic terms, the primary policy objective almost becomes maximum nature conservation. Economic analysis and discounting are used in a cost-effectiveness sense to illuminate the most efficient ways of achieving the prior environmental standards.

Leopold's "Land Ethic" plays a pivotal role in this version of the preservationist position.[17] According to one interpretation, Leopold's ideas can be viewed as an argument for a two-level criterion of ecosystem health. A conservationist criterion, which applies to particular productive systems (agricultural systems, forests, wetlands, etc.) over the duration of their exploitation, must be supplemented by a broader criterion of ecosystem health, applying to entire geographical areas. Ecosystem health requires the maintenance of biological diversity.

This criterion is difficult to put into operation. As Norton has remarked:

> because it applies holistic concepts of health to entire areas consisting of a number of interacting systems and sub-systems

and because these concepts are not yet well understood even when applied to particular ecosystems, no quantitative models exist to measure environmental health. And yet Leopold's argument has intuitive plausibility . . . .[18]

In a recent paper, Norton argues that Leopold's work significantly anticipates hierarchy theory developed by ecologists.[19] Hierarchy theorists model nature as smaller, fast-changing subsystems embedded in larger, normally slow-changing systems that encompass them.

The message for environmental management seems to be that two distinct policy stages are required. In the primary stage, limits or constraints inherent in ecological systems need to be determined. More scientific information on the fragility of the overall system is therefore urgently required. Sub-systems can be operated on the basis of resource-conservation rules derived from economic analysis, but subject to the biologically based constraints for the overall system determined in the first management stage.

(4) Abandonment of CBA *(extreme preservationist or deep ecology world-view)*

In this approach, allowance has to be made for what ethicists would call "intrinsic" or "inherent" values in nature. These are non-instrumental values – i.e. they do not necessarily provide any function or service to humans in order to be valuable. The values are "essential" – i.e. are in the assets in question rather than of human beings. Expanding the range of relevant values to intrinsic values results in what can be called the *bioethics paradigm*. The economist's difficulty with intrinsic values is that due allowance for them in practical decision-making produces stultifying rules of behaviour. Evaluating developments – e.g. a proposal to drain a wetland for agricultural use – ceases to be an issue of comparing costs and benefits (the unmodified BCA approach) or of debiting the development with the costs of creating alternative environmental assets of equal value (the modified BCA approach). Rather, it becomes one of maximizing the sum of instrumental and intrinsic values, or some variant of this rule. One such variant would be to "elevate" intrinsic value above instrumental value so that human society has to operate with technologies and products which use only the minimum of resources in order not to deplete intrinsic value more than is absolutely necessary. Such minimum intrinsic depletion rules risk wholly inequitable "trades", such as conserving intrinsic values now at the expenses of social justice – and even survival, if the context is that of poor developing countries.

Conclusions

The essential contrast, then, is between a modified CBA approach – the conservationist and sustainability paradigm – which allows for sustainability in the sense of intergenerational equity, and the preservationist bioethics paradigm, which expands the objective function to be maximized to instrumental plus intrinsic values. Endless variations on these paradigms occur. The most notable is the "strong" bioethics view, or "deep ecology", which appears to raise the "worth" of intrinsic values above that of instrumental values.[20]

There seems to be very little prospect of relaxing the modified economics paradigm to embrace wholly the bioethics paradigm. However, it can be argued that the *incidental* effect of employing a constant natural assets rule is to protect the very values that are of concern to the bioethicists. By protecting habitats, ozone layers, water quality, etc., we protect the values that the bioethicists believe are in nature. Conservation of species, for example, entails conservation of habitats, which in turn entails the avoidance of biogeographical "islands".

Deep ecologists will find this stance unacceptable, since the moral ground, in their view, rests with those who intend to behave morally, not with those who happen to secure moral outcomes because they pursue other rules of behaviour. This claim to the moral high ground is rejected because of our belief that bioethics is consistent with the sacrifice of basic human values, including fundamental rights to exist at an acceptable standard of living. In short, we argue for the modified economic paradigm as a means of integrating economic efficiency and intergenerational equity. Our further belief is that the resulting "constant natural assets" rule has two incidental effects: (i) it protects the environments of the poorest communities in the world who depend directly on those environments for fuel, water and food; and (ii) it protects the environments of sentient non-humans and non-sentient things.

Notes

1. See, for example, World Commission on Environment and Development, *Our Common Future*, Oxford University Press, Oxford, 1987; D.W. Pearce, A. Markandya and E. Barbier, *Blueprint For a Green Economy*, Earthscan, London, 1989 and R.K. Turner (ed.), *Sustainable Environmental Management: Principles and Practice*, Belhaven Press, London, 1988.
2. World Commission on Environment and Development, 1987, op. cit.
3. See T. O'Riordan and R.K. Turner, *An Annotated Reader in Environmental Planning and Management*, Pergamon Press, Oxford, 1983; B.G. Norton. "Intergenerational Equity and Environmental Decisions: A Model Using Rawls' Veil of Ignorance", *Ecological Economics*, 1, 1989, pp. 137–59; and D.W. Pearce and R.K. Turner, *Economics of Natural Resources and the Environment*, Harvester Wheatsheaf, Hemel Hempstead, 1990.
4. Many environmental resources possess the characteristics of public-type goods – i.e. excluding resource users is difficult or impossible (open access) and one individual's consumption of the good does not affect another's consumption at all.
5. P. Streeten, "What do we owe the future?" *Resources Policy*, vol. 12, no. 1, 1986, pp. 4–16.
6. By traditional ethics we mean those based on most forms of utilitarianism and libertarianism. Neither utilitarianism (i.e. that an act or rule is to be judged most desirable if it maximizes either average or total utility, even if some individuals, the minority, lose out) nor libertarianism (i.e. an action is desirable or right as long as the individual involved has legitimate entitlement or claim to support the action) can support an ethical basis for principles of intra- and intergenerational fairness requiring equal treatment for all persons.
7. The contractarian approach is based on actual or hypothetical negotiations which are said to be capable of yielding mutually

agreeable principles of conduct, which are also binding upon all parties. John Rawls has formulated an idealized decision model in order to produce procedural rules for a just society – see J. Rawls, *A Theory of Justice*, Oxford University Press, Oxford, 1972.

8. J. Penn, "Towards an Ecologically-based Society: A Rawlsian Perspective", *Ecological Economics*, 2, 1990, pp. 225–42.

9. Brandt Commission, *North-South: A Programme for Survival*, Pan, London, 1980; and Brandt Commission, *Common Crisis*, Pan, London, 1983.

10. R.K. Turner, "Sustainable Global Futures: Common Interest, Interdependency, Complexity and Global Possibilities", *Futures*, 578–84, 1987.

11. In fact the very first generation would have to save and would make this sacrifice for no reward; all future generations would get an inheritance as well as a savings burden.

12. In fact the dual nature of Rawls's Theory – justice as rational co-operation and justice as hypothetical universal assent – produces conflicts as soon as the analysis moves away from the self-contained society of contemporaries. Preservationist advocates would want the veil of ignorance conditions further modified – e.g. to take away the knowledge that the rational chooser would be an actual person and not merely a possible person; the rational chooser should also not limit what species he/she presents – see B.G. Norton (1989), op. cit.

13. T. Page, "Intergenerational Justice as Opportunity", in D. Maclean and P. Brown (eds), *Energy and the Future*, Rowman and Littlefield, Totowa, 1982.

14. What is proposed is that future generations are owed compensation for any reduction (caused by the current generation) in their access to easily extracted and conveniently located natural resources. If justice is to prevail, the future's loss of productive potential must be compensated for. Compensation is paid by the current generation via technological innovation and research and development expenditure designed to offset the impacts of depletion.

15. See Chapter 1 for definitions of these components of total economic value.

16. It has been argued that only items that have interests can be regarded as having moral or legal standing. Such interests would be capable of being represented in legal proceedings or moral debates. But now we have to define what we mean by "interests". Some philosophers have argued that to have interests requires some level of consciousness. Others have argued that virtually any

sentient thing has interests. Sentience is the capacity for feeling – pain, for example. So pain-avoidance behaviour is in the interest of the thing.

17. A. Leopold, *Sand County Almanac*, Oxford University Press, Oxford, 1949; and B.G. Norton. (1989) op. cit.

18. B.G. Norton (1989) op. cit.

19. B.G. Norton, "Context and Hierarchy in Aldo Leopold's Theory of Environmental Management", *Ecological Economics*, 2, 1990, pp. 119–27.

20. A. Naess, "The Shallow and the Deep, Long Range Ecology Movement: A Summary", *Inquiry*, vol. 16, no. 1, 1973, pp. 95–100.

Epigraph

The kingdom of plants and animals is near at hand; though Man forgets his Maker, plants and animals are very near the light. And Poet, tell men that love is born with the same exaltation in all planes of life – that the rhythm of a leaf swaying in the wind is the same as that of a distant star, and that the very words spoken by the fountain in the shade are repeated by the sea, and in the same tone. Tell Man to be humble. In nature, all things are equal.

(Federico Garcia Lorca, Prologue to *The Butterfly's Evil Spell*)

Index